KAY N. SANECKI

P9-BIF-018

Discovering
Herbs

SHIRE PUBLICATIONS LTD

Contents

Front cover: A corner of the herb garden at Castle Drogo, Devon, where, as in many other herb gardens, decorative forms of herb are grown. *Monarda didyma* 'Croftway Pink' is not a true herb.

British Library Cataloguing in Publication Data
Sanecki, Kay N.
  Discovering herbs.—4th ed.—(Discovering
series; no. 89)
  1. Herbs
  I. Title
  641.3'57   SB351.H5
  ISBN 0-85263-719-5

Copyright © 1970 and 1985 by Kay N. Sanecki. First published 1970. Second edition 1973; reprinted 1976 and 1978. Third edition, 1982. Fourth edition 1985, reprinted 1988. Number 89 in the Discovering series. ISBN 0 85263 719 5.

Set in 9 on 9 point English Times by Permanent Typesetting & Printing Co Ltd, Hong Kong, and printed in Great Britain by C. I. Thomas & Sons (Haverfordwest) Ltd, Merlins Bridge, Haverfordwest.

1. A place for herbs

To most people the word *herb* seems to conjure up some delight of the palate, almost a mental taste, confused with a sweet aroma. Our forefathers indeed used plants to add flavour, to vary flavour or to mask putrefaction of food, and some herbs are still commonly employed in traditional practices. With regard to their medicinal use the story is somewhat different, for herbalism as such was practised by ancient civilisations and the Anglo-Saxon word *dregen,* to dry, is the source of the word *drug.* Much of our acceptance of the medicinal action of plants is traditional and herbal practice employs the simple methods that have sufficed for generations. The early herbalists were botanists; the early botanists wrote and illustrated the herbals – some of the earliest books to be produced in Europe – and, inevitably, botany and medicine stem from twin courses. The great schism came during the seventeenth and eighteenth centuries when folk remedies were frequently employed alongside the newly established orthodox medicine, and a herbalist was frequently an apothecary or a barber surgeon. The general flow of population towards the towns in the nineteenth century meant that many people were deprived of the proximity of their known remedies and clung to the few tried and tested plants available for sale, sometimes under cover, while the traditional remedies were, for the great part, perpetuated among the rural communities. As orthodox medicine developed it drew on traditional knowledge and many established drugs of today are plant products. It is noteworthy that the poisonous drug extracts like belladonna, digitalis, aconite and stramonium are employed in orthodox medicine. In the urban communities herbalism became a shadowy cult until its revival at the beginning of the present century, and today there is an ever strengthening interest in the 'natural' remedy.

The English names of plants often suggest the use to which the plant was put in former times, such as throatwort, bladderwort, eyebright, lungwort – the word *wort* meaning plant – and long after the plant had fallen into disuse the name lives on. The specific Latin name *officinalis* means that this is the species employed medicinally, or officially.

Today the greatest interest is taken in herbs for culinary delight, for winemaking and for sweet-smelling qualities. There is an undeniable fascination in growing something of old-world charm and association, especially when it can be reinstated in modern guise as a condiment. The English names are used throughout this book; in chapter 5 the Latin names are given for clarity of identification. The modern vogue for collecting something – anything it would seem – cannot be more delightfully engaged upon than by making a collection of growing plants that have folklore associations through the centuries and yet provide useful material and interest. Suggestions for growing and using these plants are given in later pages, without any reference to the legends and myths that surround them – these can be sought elsewhere – and the emphasis is on cultivating herbs.

2. Plan to grow herbs

The beginner need not be deterred from starting to grow herbs by lack of horticultural know-how or by meagre funds. To attain some measure of success two factors are essential: a suitable soil and some shelter from prevailing winds.

Soil

The first condition is best fulfilled by choosing plants that will either like or tolerate the type of soil rather than by making a sustained effort to change the nature of the soil, and provided that the site is not waterlogged or badly drained some herbs can be grown. A heavy clay soil is the least suitable for herbs, and mint is probably the only culinary herb that can be expected to flourish, but much can be done to ameliorate the condition of such a soil and lighten its texture. This is achieved by the addition of compost, peat, hops and other humus-encouraging materials. A clay soil, light in texture and well managed, is perfectly suited to the cultivation of herbs. At the other end of the scale, a very light sandy, hungry soil also needs humus in the form of compost, peat and leaf mould to improve its moisture-retentive qualities and until this can be achieved only those herbs that flourish in baked soils, like rosemary, marjoram and thymes, can be expected to thrive properly.

Thus, on whatever soil herbs are to be grown, the preparation of the land, to bring it into good heart, is the first essential and time and money used in this way are well spent. Clear perennial weeds by forking out and an application of a residual weed killer in autumn will help to keep the land free of annual weeds the following spring. Lightly fork in compost, or whatever humus-producing material is available during the autumn, and let the hard weather do the remainder of the work.

Compost is derived from vegetable waste, both kitchen scraps and garden material: weeds, potato and pea haulms, lawn mowings, hedge clippings and the like. Layers of this material should alternate with layers of good garden soil and a sprinkling

4

of a proprietary compost activator, to form a compost heap. A wire mesh bin can be filled in layers and the contents left to rot and break down to a brown crumbly texture for some six months before being forked on to the land to provide organic material.

Organic fertilisers include bonemeal or boneflour, hoof and horn and dried blood, and inorganic fertilisers (strictly the so called 'artificials') are manufactured products of known chemical content usually sold as granules or pellets. In general, herbs do not require the balanced and controlled feeding obtainable from this type of fertiliser except in a few instances where the plant needs a fillip to recover after a crop has been taken.

Shelter

Herbs are always at their best in warm still air and protection from the prevailing winds is essential, although any shelter provided should not plunge the herb border into shade. It is a good idea to plant a herb hedge, of rosemary, sage, artemisia, lavender or roses, and while these are growing some measure of temporary windbreak can be provided quickly by growing annual sunflowers. The long-term plan of growing a hedge to surround a herb garden is justified because the seclusion will prevent drying winds from robbing the plants of their aromatic qualities and a completeness of design will be achieved.

Starting a herb garden

Some herbs are raised annually from seed sown in the early months of the year: chervil, dill, summer savory, basil, caraway, borage, parsley, purslane and corn salad. Seed can be bought cheaply or saved from the previous summer and needs to be sown in March in pots or boxes, thinned, hardened off and planted out of doors in May; or sown directly into the ground in drills during April and May. Make two sowings of such plants as purslane and corn salad to ensure a succession of fresh young leaves. If the drill for parsley is watered with very hot water immediately before sowing the period of germination will be shortened, for parsley seed is notoriously slow to germinate. One or two herbs, notably angelica, verbascum, clary sage, woad and evening primrose, are biennials. That is, they are sown one year, usually in summer, to flower the following one. Several biennials appear to behave like perennials once they are established, especially if the flowering stems are cut away and the plants are not allowed to form seed. Other plants, like borage, marigolds and fennel, sow themselves so easily that their effect is perennial.

Most of the perennial herbs, such as chicory, comfrey and lemon balm, can also be raised from seed although vegetative propagation from divisions, offsets or cuttings is sometimes less hazardous. Tarragon, chives, marjoram and mint can be divided easily in spring. Cuttings of rosemary, lavender and santolina can be struck, in a frame, in spring or, if made with a heel of old wood, in the open, in July. (This involves tearing away a small strip of the old wood at the base of the cutting, so that a sprig of the present season's growth has a tag of last year's growth attached to it.) Put cuttings into a sandy compost in a box, frame or open land and protect them from sunshine. Young roots will form soon in most cases and the rooted cuttings can be planted out in the autumn or the following spring.

In the list of herbs in chapter 5 each plant is described as annual, biennial or perennial to guide the amateur in the general pattern of their cultivation and propagation.

Renovating an old herb garden

Worn-out or scraggy plants are best thrown out, and after the ground has been forked over and cleared of creeping roots and perennial weeds a fresh supply of plants can be sown or planted.

Lavender bushes that have become leggy and bare need to be grubbed out and rooted cuttings can be planted out to replace them, but where sage or thyme has grown straggly build up a mound of good garden soil or potting compost around them, making it firm and leaving only the tips of the shoots protruding. Roots will form quite quickly along the covered stems at the leaf joints and these shoots can be severed and replanted tidily, and the old foundation plants discarded. Frequently a neglected herb garden looks much worse than it need because the hedges have become overgrown or unproductive at the base. Rose hedges can be cut right back to within a few inches of the ground and will break again, and box and santolina can be clipped right back with sharp shears. The new leafy growth will soon thicken up the hedge.

Many of the larger nurseries stock the generally cultivated herbs, and some garden centres have plentiful supplies in the spring. But there are good nurseries that specialise in herbs and herb products from which the more unusual plants and collec-tor's items can be purchased (listed at the back of this book). There is also a growing number of specialist seedsmen specialis-ing in wild flower, old vegetables and herbs seeds; their catalogues make exciting reading. It is always advisable to obtain both plants and seed from a reliable source and any herb nursery or farm that is a member of The British Herb Trade Association can be relied upon to provide good clean stock. Furthermore, for the most part, they have the plants properly identified.

Many herbs are European natives, including Britain, and there is perhaps a temptation to collect plants from the wild. Under the Conservation of Wild Creatures and Wild Plants Act,

1975, it is an offence, with a fine of up to £100 upon conviction, for anyone, without permission of the owner or occupier of the land, to dig up plants in the countryside. This refers to any wild plant, not just the twenty-one scheduled species which are totally protected by the Act.

What to grow

The selection of plants to include in a herb garden is a personal decision depending on site, available space and requirements.

Culinary herbs such as a cook might prefer to include are mint, sage, parsley, chives, basil, tarragon, caraway, rosemary, lovage and salad crops like dandelion, nasturtium and corn salad. Only a small number of plants is needed for such a collection because only a few leaves at a time are gathered unless the plants are to be dried and stored for winter use, in which case more will be required.

Decorative herbs can be assembled in a more extensive collection, to include a representative array wherein the officinal, culinary and decorative plants of old-world association can be grown together. Here one could include tansy, rosemary, roses, bergamot, catmint, foxglove, lily-of-the-valley, poppy, sunflower and many others.

Medicinal herbs or herbs of healing would include many wild flowers, as these were the first simples known to our ancestors and some such as coltsfoot should be introduced with care as they can be invasive. Sink an old bucket or plastic bowl and plant these wandering types in it to waylay the travelling rootstocks and confine the growth without too much hard work. Selfheal, pulmonaria, raspberry, horehound, coltsfoot, hyssop, comfrey, foxglove, feverfew and agrimony would each merit inclusion in a medicinal collection.

Sweet-smelling herbs for the scented garden can be classified in two ways: those that give off their perfume into the air or some that need the merest brush of the hand to encourage them to loosen their aroma; and those that are less generous and need to be crushed or bruised to release their scent. Many cottage garden plants fall into the first category: pinks, wallflowers, lilac, daphne, honeysuckle, stocks, narcissi, violets, lily-of-the-valley, heliotrope and roses. Among those that need encouragement to exhale their perfume are tansy, nasturtium, marigold, thyme, chamomile, box, pelargonium, rosemary, lavender, rue, mint, salvia, bergamot and artemisia.

A natural order garden probably appeals to the gardener of botanical inclination, each bed housing plants within the same natural order. These can be interesting but are of insignificant decorative value. The plants belonging to, say, *Labiatae,* such as salvia, rosemary, marjoram and hyssop, can be grouped together and in another bed the compositous plants such as colts-foot, chicory and sunflower. The *Umbelliferae* collection would include fennel, dill, caraway and parsley. In chapter 5 the natural order of each plant is recorded not only for the purpose of description but to guide the beginner with ideas for making such a collection.

Planning the herb garden

The size of the herb plot, be it kitchen border or extensively decorative garden, is again a matter of personal taste and depends largely upon the space and funds available, but the decision of long or short term planting has to be reached at the outset. Assuming one plant is allowed per square foot as a general guide, on richer soils a matured effect can be achieved in two or three years, while on the drier soils this rate of planting will give a more sparse result and will need up to four years for effect.

Borders. The less sophisticated the herb border, the better. Plants need to be assembled in groups where the texture or shape of the leaves of one kind will act as a foil for those of its neighbour, in much the same way as a herbaceous border is planned. The lower-growing plants, say thyme, chives, violets, and marigolds, need to be set towards the front of the border, the taller ones, like angelica, mullein and sage, to the back. Some form of background is necessary. If it is provided by a wall, then roses, jasmine or honeysuckle can be trained over it; or shrubs or a hedge can form the background. Roses, bay, the rough-leaved sage and box are all suitable. Refrain from the temptation of using privet or elder as the background hedge; while both grow rapidly and provide flowers redolent in their season, they will impoverish the border by their foraging roots.

The border can be planned formally, setting the plants either in rectangular blocks or in wedge-shaped sections arranged fanwise. In both instances the proportions are important and for attractive results the border should be fairly wide and not a long narrow strip of ground.

Formal designs. No one would describe herbs as first-class plants where good garden effect is required and thus by using them in a repeated theme complemented by the bold design of formal-shaped beds the best herb gardens are designed. Based upon either a circle or a rectangle of varying proportions, a series of interesting plants can be evolved. The simplest is to imitate the rim and spokes of a wheel, marking them out in a box, santolina or pinks, and to fill the 'wedges' between each spoke with contrasting plants. The central hub of the wheel can be emphasised by a sundial, birdbath, seat, beehive or standard plant, such as a rose or honeysuckle. Essentially, the 'wheel' must not be too small.

Planned along straight lines, rather than curves or arcs, the square or rectangular enclosed garden lends itself best as a herb or aromatic garden. Beds should be large enough not to give a dotted effect and yet small enough to be workable. Perhaps the edges can be traced in some plant such as pinks, santolina, lavender or box, related to the size of the bed itself and to the garden in general. Individual beds can be planned to hold a number of herbs, each of which ought to be planted in more than one bed to bring the design together as a whole. Or the individual beds could be planted entirely with one plant or one group of plants – culinary, dye, medicinal, folklore, still room, strewing or nosegay. Another idea is to confine plants of a coloured foliage into one bed, say silver-grey leaved plants such as some artemisias, lavender cotton, lavender, sage, curry plant, mullein, camphor plant, eucalyptus, horehound, sea holly and thymes such as *Thymus* × *citriodorus* 'Silver Queen' and *Thymus vulgaris* 'Silver Posie'. Dark or purple-leaved plants could be collected together; they would be fennel in the bronze-leaved form, the purple sage, peppermint, wall germander, basil 'Dark Opal', black horehound and juniper.

The chequerboard design is a favourite for a herb collection, where small square beds are formed in staggered rows, each devoted to an individual plant. The same theme can be used less formally where patches of herbs are tucked into spaces between the paving stones of a patio or terrace and to good effect if the thymes, pennyroyal, mints and chamomile are used, as they emit their fragrance when crushed underfoot. A pavement or path garden can be used to cover a large or small area, thus providing a useful thoroughfare in the garden and at the same time a near trouble-free herb garden.

The most elaborately designed herb garden is one made along the lines of an Elizabethan knot garden and based upon an intricate pattern of beds, each outlined by clipped box or santolina. Designs can vary from rectangular beds to intricate decorative curves emulating the outline of leaves, but the constant factor is that the design is repetitive and is intended to be regarded as a whole and from above or afar to be enjoyed as a parterre.

Where more extensive gardens are planned a carefully selected tree or trees can be included. Suggestions are rowan, mulberry, magnolia, calycanthus, lime, witch hazel, eucalyptus, elder or bay.

Growing herbs in confined spaces

Not everyone who wishes to cultivate a few herbs has a garden or even space to spare in the garden, but many herbs, particularly the culinary ones, are accommodating in that they will thrive in confined root runs and so can be expected to grow quite happily in tubs, pots and window boxes.

Innumerable gardens simply do not have appropriate areas where herbs can be cultivated, lacking light or shelter or perhaps having only a heavy soil. By cultivating herbs and aromatic plants in containers, they can be moved to a sunny spot or taken elsewhere once their most interesting season is over. Pots can be sunk into a border, to rim level, and changed from time to time according to how the plants are doing and what else in the garden is in flower.

Containers can be window boxes, tubs, troughs, pots or even a purpose-built low wall, of brick or stone, where plants can be grown along the top. Such a wall is a most acceptable edge to a patio or acts as a division between one part of the garden and another. Where herbs are to be grown in any of these ways it is a good idea to consider them only as summer plants, using the containers for something else like bulbs or spring bedding plants at other periods of the year. The trick is to plant rooted cuttings of herbs into the containers, or those little plants that can be purchased from garden centres, their roots encased in black plastic bags. Containers should be filled with compost, and the small plants tucked in. Move the arrangement of bags around before actually planting so that a pleasing assembly results. Be prepared to remove any plant that outgrows the proportions of its container or grows out of proportion with its neighbours, for the trick of container-grown herbs is to plant closely and treat them as though they are intended to be temporary residents. Remember that during warm weather containers of all kinds need special attention from the watering can.

Some suggestions are:

Troughs: thymes, chives, rooted cuttings of bay, rosemary and chamomile.

Window boxes: basil, especially 'Dark Opal', bay, chives, corn salad, feverfew, lavender cotton, lungwort, marjoram, nasturtium, parsley, rue, tarragon and thymes.

Tubs: bay, chives, feverfew, lavender cotton, lungwort, nasturtium, parsley, lavender, rosemary, tarragon, wall germander, artemisias, lemon balm, hyssop, fennel, mint and sage.

Indoors: lemon verbena, pineapple sage, parsley, rosemary, marjoram, bush basil (especially in autumn when it has finished in the garden), thymes, mint (in water) and chives.

In walls: catmint, chamomile, feverfew, horehound, lungwort, rue, marjoram, thymes, houseleek, sea holly, lavender cotton, curry plant, sages, especially the purple and tricolor forms, hyssop, savories and marigolds.

3. Harvesting

Having grown the herbs, it is essential to know which part of the plant is required – leaves, seeds or root – and when it is ready for harvesting. Information as to the part of the plant used is easily acquired but knowing exactly when to harvest to advantage takes a little practical experience. The general rule for cutting leaves is to do so just as the flowers come to be fully opened, because this is the apogee of the plant's annual metabolism and the active principle in the herb is at its strongest at this time. Roots and seeds should be taken on maturity. It is important to collect the right part of the plant because the active elements are not necessarily present in other parts of the same plant and indeed there are some instances where one part of the plant may be edible and another poisonous: for example, the tubers of the potato are staple food, but the fruits are poisonous.

Collecting roots

Roots need to be lifted carefully with a garden fork or flat-tined potato fork and rubbed or washed free of soil. Autumn is the time to lift roots, when the top growth begins to die back, for then the roots are mature.

Leaves

Individual leaves can be taken from such culinary plants as mint, sage, parsley, rosemary, basil and bay as and when required; or whole young shoots can be removed without detriment to the plant. But to remove a crop of leaves for drying and preserving for winter use is an operation of greater importance and needs subtle timing. Pick whole shoots without rendering an individual plant incapable of carrying on its normal function of flowering or seeding – unless of course the plants are being cleared and have been grown solely for the supply of this season's harvest of leaves. The leaves that are gathered need to be free of insects and disease and dry, and often a gentle shake early in the day will rid them of dew quite quickly and hasten the completely dry condition. The most satisfactory stage at which to collect leaves is just as the flowers are coming to maturity.

Flowers

As soon as a flower is fully open it is at its best. Its colour and perfume are then strongest and the petals unblemished. More of the essential oils can be captured at this time and if lavender and rosemary flowers can be collected the day before they are fully open, so much the better, as the colour will persist more certainly, but only the practised eye can recognise this stage. It is very

11

important that bruising of petals and crushing of flowerheads is avoided.

Whole herb

In some instances all the above-ground parts of a plant are cut and this is usually carried out when the plant is about to flower because it is then at maximum efficiency and at its most useful as an active herb. Sometimes several cuttings are required and some can be taken before the first flowering and others later in the season when secondary bushy growth has been produced as a direct result of the first harvesting. Sage, savory and marjoram can be treated in this way. Secateurs can be used, though the operation is necessarily slow, and where a fair quantity of the crop is to be gathered a sharp linoleum knife is a most effective tool and can be used to slash the plant cleanly right back to older growth. Bushy plants like sage, thyme and rosemary can be neatly cut back to the previous year's growth and the work can proceed fairly quickly because the fresh young growth is quite soft and easily cut away. Knives used for this purpose must be kept sharp not only for effectiveness but to prevent tearing the growth.

Seed

Sometimes seed is collected for use and at other times for propagation to maintain stocks of the plants the following year. When it is destined for sowing it should be allowed to ripen as far as possible and be collected only from typical well grown plants. When seed is being taken from plants for culinary use, for example from dill or caraway, the plants can be pulled up and hung upside down with a paper bag tied over the old flowerhead to catch the seeds as they fall from the dried placenta. Do not be tempted to use plastic bags for this purpose, easier though it may be to be able to keep an eye on progress. Porous paper bags are far more likely to preserve the precious harvest. It is sometimes difficult to judge the time at which seed will be ready — a couple of hot days encourage the plant to scatter its seeds seemingly prematurely. Muslin bags popped over the whole inflorescence and tied with string or rubber bands will catch the escaping seeds, and later the stem can be cut below the neck of the bag and the seeds emptied on to paper indoors. Often holidays or periods away from the garden coincide with the time of ripening seeds and by covering the seed heads with paper bags many otherwise elusive seeds can be collected. Seed being saved for propagation needs to be carefully labelled and stored in a cool dry shaded place in paper bags, pill boxes or envelopes of aluminium foil.

Bark

Occasionally the bark contains the active element of the plant and is used especially to provide some plant alkaloids and dyes.

Homeopathic medicine usually indicates at what time of the year bark ought to be collected from the various trees and shrubs recognised as drug plants, and it is usually in the spring or autumn that the bark must be carefully shaved off the branches and dried. Collecting bark from trees growing in the wild is not to be encouraged and great patches of branch should never be left bare or the tree will suffer as a consequence.

4. Drying

Drying is the most important operation in the successful culture of herbs and the time and expense of careful cultivation can be forfeited in a matter of hours if the drying process is inadequately or inefficiently carried out. Much of the value of the plant can be lost by hurried or ineffective drying, and for medicinal purposes, certainly, there ought to be a minimum accepted amount of the active alkaloid or glucodine in a given sample of dried material. No herb can be stored fresh; a few can be preserved for culinary use by deep freezing (see later), but the material can be utterly valueless unless it is carefully dealt with after harvesting.

The housewife who wishes to keep a few sprigs of mint, sage, rosemary, chervil, basil, bay and tarragon for winter use can dry freshly collected leaves in a constantly warm airing cupboard, spare bedroom, airy loft or garden shed in open boxes or on sheets of paper, but for any quantity in excess of the small domestic requirements special facilities are necessary. Avoid using kitchens and bathrooms as there is normally too much moisture in the air from cooking and washing. Plants such as sage and thyme can be hung from rafters or on cords stretched across a dry, dust-free room. The bunches should be composed of a few sprigs only and fastened loosely by the stems to allow air to circulate.

An empty greenhouse or a section of the greenhouse screened off by plastic sheeting hung as a temporary partition can provide good conditions. Shade should be given by blinds or a fly sheet or even by sheets of newspaper. Soil beds in the greenhouse need covering with plastic sheeting to prevent the evaporation of moisture from the soil and the ventilation needs to be controlled to maintain a buoyant atmosphere.

A clean wooden garden shed or summer house can be used for drying small quantities of herbs but one is dependent then upon sun heat, and the natural fluctuation in temperature with the consequent change in moisture content of the atmosphere discourages even drying.

Drying rooms

Where anything other than a small quantity of material is to be dried it is necessary to provide a sufficiently warm atmosphere with adequate heat and ventilation to maintain dryness in spite of the water being drawn off from the plant material. In addition to this, enough space is required to deal with the bulk of material likely to be harvested at any one time, and some means of providing shade from the daylight is needed. Herbs tend to be bleached when dried in sunlight. A drying room is something to consider if one is dealing with herbs in any quantity or engaged in the cultivation of herbs for market.

Some form of heating is required, capable of maintaining an equable temperature of 90F (32C), and some form of ventilation to keep the air moving. Water vapour is present in air; the warmer the air the more moisture it can contain and this must be moved away because the faster that dry air can be brought to the plant material the more evenly will the material dry. An extractor fan set high in the room often provides the solution. A common mistake for beginners to make is to introduce freshly gathered plant material into a warm room where herbs are almost dry. The initial moisture drawn from the fresh material is reabsorbed by the dry herbs from the atmosphere. If new material has to be brought into the room before the process has been completed it should be placed high up in the room and for this reason, as well as to be economical of space, plant material is best dealt with in trays stacked in racks. The trays themselves can be made from wooden frames with a cross-piece set in each corner to prevent twisting, over which hessian, butter muslin, old terylene curtains or old sheets are stretched and secured by drawing pins. The trays should be of a size not too unwieldy to handle and can be slung on a series of 'hammocks' set across the room or slotted into racks used for the purpose. Naturally, if racks are used these will determine the dimensions of the trays. Permanent shelving is not advisable because air must be able to circulate around the trays. It is always wise to have all the racks and trays the same size so that trays can be changed from one position in the room to another.

Drying

It is wise to harvest only the quantity of clean material that can be dealt with the same day and to label each kind of herb carefully to avoid confusion once they are dried; and always keep one plant separate from another. The material should be spread out quite thinly on the trays and during the first two days turned frequently. Get the room sufficiently warm before harvesting and the initial high temperature during the first twenty-four hours of the drying process needs to be 90-95F (32-34C) to reduce the water content of the plant as quickly as possible before any deterioration starts. The moisture content of most plants is well above seventy per cent and the aim is brisk drying without shrivelling to change the condition of the leaf rather than its chemical content. As the water content is relatively high a considerable bulk of fresh material is needed to provide an adequate supply of the dried product. A broad estimate is that 8 pounds of freshly harvested plant material will provide 1 pound of dried herb.

After the first twenty-four hours, the temperature can be reduced to 75 or 80F (25 or 27C) to finish off the process evenly without blackening the leaves. The whole process usually takes three to six days. Dryness can be judged by breaking stems between the finger and thumb, and when the process is complete they should snap crisply. Roots need to be tested with a knife and need to be dry right through; if a spongy core remains they will soon rot. Should the drying process be incomplete, moisture will be reabsorbed from the atmosphere, the herbs will smell musty and will soon be mouldy.

Rubbing down

As soon as the herbs are dry and have cooled down some arrangement must be made to store them and, if they are destined for sale, to transport them. Sacks should not be stacked on the floor but are better hung to allow the free movement of air around them. The rubbing-down process needs to be done in good ventilation, probably wearing gloves and certainly a smog mask as protection against the dust produced during the operation. Domestic amounts of material can be dealt with satisfactorily by hand-picking the leaves, discarding the stalks and crushing the leaves first with a rolling pin and subsequently rubbing them through a fine sieve. Larger quantities may need to be milled in a coffee grinder or domestic mixer once the stalks and chaff have been removed by hand. It is at this stage that one discovers that the leaves were sandy or dirty before drying! For even larger amounts some form of chaff cutter is used but most herbs can be marketed whole after drying, and to deal with these large quantities is a commercial concern.

Storing herbs

The amounts of most domestic preserves are gauged to provide a continuous supply throughout the winter, and herbs are no exception. There is little point in storing large quantities, although attractively packed samples make useful Christmas presents.

Label each kind of herb and store it in some airtight container so that it cannot reabsorb moisture from the atmosphere. Small glass jars with screw tops can be used but ought to be kept in a cupboard away from the light. Wooden boxes or decorative wooden drums make a pleasing alternative. For a short period of time plastic bags may be used, sealed either by using a warm iron or with the wire and paper strips provided with the bags to keep them as airtight as possible. Never use tins for dried herbs.

Freezing

Most culinary herbs can be frozen reasonably satisfactorily, although naturally they are not crisp and fresh when they are brought out and therefore not as useful for garnishing. Those that are floppy or filmy of foliage, such as dill or fennel, are best mixed with other herbs in a suitable combination before freezing, so that they can be used together: say, dill with parsley and chives, for use in sauces: or tarragon and chervil, to flavour egg dishes.

Cut the sprigs of herbs when they are dry, and take only a small amount at a time. Wash them free of grit if necessary and dry thoroughly, then pack in polythene bags and label clearly. Alternatively, freeze small sprigs of flavouring herbs in ice cubes and store, then add to stews and casseroles immediately from the freezer while cooking is in progress. A more reliable method of preservation for most herbs is to blanch quickly before freezing, that is to dip them into boiling water for just a minute before putting into the freezer bags. The satisfactory freezer life for herbs that have been blanched is five or six months. It is less for herbs that have not been blanched.

5. Some herbs to grow

The following catalogue of herbs includes suggestions for various types of collections of herbs. Notes are given as to whether the plant is annual or perennial to provide a guide to cultivation. Some plants included are poisonous and the need to educate children to recognise them cannot be overstressed.

Agrimony *Agrimonia eupatoria* (Rosaceae)   Perennial
Yellow agrimony, church steeples

Agrimony is a common hedgerow plant all over Britain, especially on porous soils where it can find a sun-baked spot. The pretty fern-like leaves make a tisane, when infused, fragrant of apricots. The whole plant is faintly aromatic (even the root, especially in spring) and retains the fragrance when dried. The tiny yellow flowers are massed on a slender spike, the lower flowers blooming first, and have earned the plant the country name of church steeples. They are in flower from July onwards, until the cool days come.

The whole plant yields a yellow dye, rather pale from late summer plants, but deepening as the weeks pass in the autumn. Propagation is from seed, which is available from nurseries and seedsmen specialising in wild plants.

Alecost *Balsamita major*, Syn. *Tanacetum balsamita* (Compositae) Costmary   Perennial

The plant is commonly confused with the camphor plant (*q. v.*) but the main distinguishing feature is that costmary or alecost has yellow button flowers in July and August, whereas the flowers of the camphor plant are white and daisy-like.

The leaves are ovate, green and a little glaucous and when pressed or crushed they emit a soft balsam-mint aroma. A trace, chopped in a salad, adds a subtle flavour, or the leaves can be added, with restraint, to pot-pourri, because they hold their scent well on drying. It is a plant for a sunny spot, raised from spring-sown seed or propagated by division of roots in spring.

Alexanders *Smyrnium olisatrum* (Umbelliferae)   Perennial
Alisanders, black lovage, black pot herb

The whole plant has a yellowish green appearance. The mop heads of flowers resemble those of angelica so strongly that sometimes the two plants are confused. But this plant grows wild in coastal areas, particularly in the south-west of England, and is noticeable early in the season, especially in April, for its lush pale growth which seems so far in advance of all other plants. The stout stems quickly reach some 3 to 4 feet (0.9–1.2 m) in height and, when young, afford a celery-flavoured addition to casseroles and soups. The flowers are fragrant, and the leaves large, shining and deeply divided.

Allium *see* Garlic

Allspice *Calycanthus floridus* (Calycanthaceae)   Tree or shrub

This tree of small proportions bears in August curious brownish crimson flowers that resemble little bunches of ribbons because the petals are strap-shaped. Every part of the tree is aromatic, rich and spicy. Although this is not a herb, it makes a very attractive and fragrant addition to a sheltered herb garden. Flowers, bark and wood can be included in small amounts in pot-pourri.

Native to the southern United States, this plant is not the source of commercial allspice, which comes from the berries of an evergreen tree native to the West Indies, Central and South America and which is most prolifically grown in Jamaica and has come to be called Jamaica pepper.

Angelica *Angelica archangelica* (Umbelliferae)　　　　Perennial

Botanically angelica is a biennial, but seedlings make slow progress the first summer, sometimes flowering the second or third year after sowing and dying after flowering. But the plants sow their seed about the garden, so once introduced angelica will always be at home. Where plants are prevented from flowering and are used for their attractive stalks, they will tend to live on. This is a pity because their large many-spoked mop-head flowers from June to September are a dramatic feature of any garden. So it is necessary to decide to what purpose angelica is to be put in the garden.

Cultivated mainly for its young green stems, which can be candied and used in confectionery, it is a marvellous plant for the back of the border or for a corner, where height is needed. Provide it with some shelter from the wind, so that it can give of its best. Medium damp good garden loam is suitable, where there is shade at some time of the day or day-long dappled shade.

Grow from spring-sown seed, or transplant self-sown seedlings to a salient position in May.

Anise *Pimpinella anisum* (Umbelliferae)　　　　Annual

Anise is a dainty half-hardy annual plant, with feathery leaves and tiny white flowers in summer. Its round aromatic seed, well known for flavouring liqueurs, medicine and confectionery, will ripen sufficiently in Britain only in good summers and where the plants are grown in warm sheltered localities. Cut down the whole plant as soon as the seed is ripe and allow it to dry off lying on newspaper in a warm dry dust-free place, so that the seed will fall. In temperate climates the seed does not get a sufficiently long growing season, so for good culinary use it is best to purchase it. Aniseed is one of the best known digestive herbs, and the flavour is sweetly penetrating and liquorice-like. Try adding just a drop of an anise-flavoured drink, such as Pernod or Ricard, to a sauce or to garlic butter to serve with shellfish. The Romans took sweetmeats strongly flavoured with anise after rich food, and the seed can be nibbled to sweeten the breath.

Artemisia *see* Southernwood and Tarragon

Balm *see* Lemon balm

Basil, Sweet *Ocimum basilicum* (Labiatae)　　　　Annual

It is not easy to get a good crop of basil in damp British summers and it is best treated as a half-hardy annual in most areas of the British Isles. Unfortunately, well established plants seem to lose the sweetness of aroma and take on a strong, rather minty-clove overtone. So the cook who knows and likes to use basil is well advised to try to maintain a supply of young plants for use in the kitchen. It loses much of its interest and unique flavour when dried but is sometimes stored by soaking leaves in good quality olive oil, packing them into a wide-necked jar, with a sprinkling of sea salt, and then filling up the jar with oil. Alternatively, a few leaves can be kept in the freezer, after being painted over with olive oil on both sides.

Sweet basil, sometimes called common basil, has larger leaves than the dwarf, bush basil (*Ocimum minimum*). The latter may be slightly hardier and can certainly be potted up at the end of the summer and grown on indoors to provide autumn leaves for the kitchen. Where frame space is available in the kitchen garden, try growing both basils there. Basil has a great affinity for tomatoes, aubergine and pâté and can be used with restraint to enhance such dishes, for those who like its clove-like flavour.

Bay *Laurus nobilis* (Lauraceae)   Tree or shrub
Sweet bay
An evergreen, enjoying a warm sheltered site, bay forms a small tree when left to its own devices, but it is frequently clipped into formal shapes and cultivated in a tub. (There are bay trees of enormous height at Margam Park, West Glamorgan, behind the orangery.) Cold winds are its principal enemy, searing the aromatic leaves. It is quite difficult to propagate, but seed can be sown in April, or layers of established plants pegged down in summer, or cuttings of young wood taken at the same period and encouraged in a small propagator or frame. The foliage sprigs dry easily when hung up in a warm atmosphere and a leaf may be used, dry or fresh, to flavour casseroles or fish dishes.

Bergamot *Monarda didyma* (Labiatae)   Perennial
Bee balm, sweet-scented balm, Oswego tea
Originally bergamot came from the swamp areas of North America, and this hints at the conditions it prefers. Sunny moist places suit it best, but where the soil is dry it requires some shade during the day. The red flowers are held around the stem in sparkler fashion and are spiky and lipped. They lend a particularly decorative air when used to garnish salads or fruit dishes. As garden plants, cultivars with variously coloured flowers are available, mauve, pink and white, in addition to the handsome reds. The foliage is aromatic and, dried well, can be infused as a pleasant tea.

Bistort *Polygonum bistorta* (Polygonaceae)   Perennial
Snakeroot, Easter ledges
Extensive colonies of bistort are to be found in the north of England and in Scotland, in areas where the plant was mainly

used in Easter pudding recipes. As a cultivated plant it is popularly used as ground cover, the whole mat of growth spiked with sugar-pink fat flowerheads from June to August. The twisted black-skinned roots are rich in tannic acid and highly astringent and can be used to stanch bleeding of wounds. Powdered root is used for this purpose. If half a pound (227 g) of root is boiled in water for about ten minutes the decoction makes an effective mouthwash or gargle. As a vegetable the leaves in early spring are spinach-like and were used along with young nettle leaves, blackcurrant leaves and parsley, mixed with barley and oatmeal and boiled in a pudding cloth. Later egg and butter were added to make an Easter pudding.

Bloodroot *Sanguinaria canadenis* (Papaveraceae)   Perennial
This is an early spring flowering plant, and the large palmate lobed leaves develop later in the season. The waxen white flowers have a cluster of golden anthers at the centre. But it is for the root that the plant is grown. It yields an orange-red dye used by the American Indians for painting their skins, and it imparts a similar colour to cloth. It is a poisonous plant and has been used in the treatment of chronic skin disorders such as varicose ulcers. Select a gravel soil for it, if possible where there is dappled shade. It grows happily in the herb garden at Acorn Bank, Cumbria.

Bog myrtle *Myrica gale* (Myricaceae)   Perennial
Sweet gale
The bog myrtle is a native plant of boggy ground, particularly fragrant during warm spells. It is quite difficult to establish but will flourish in acid boggy swampland where all other plants fail. It is well worth trying on the borders of a bog garden or planted in some old container, which can be kept soggy, sunk into a border. The plant may be divided in spring, once it starts to grow. It forms a close bush some 2 feet (0.6 m) high and bears inconspicuous flowers. A spice made from the ground dried leaves can be used as flavouring for sauces and gravies and for risotto.
The wax myrtle, *Myrica cerifera,* is a North American evergreen shrub and the glaucous wax which encrusts the bluish fruits that cling to the stems can be made into fragrantly burning candles. For this reason it is sometimes known as candleberry. The foliage yields a yellow dye.

Borage *Borago officinalis* (Boraginaceae)   Annual
A hardy annual, the entire borage plant is rough with white, somewhat prickly hairs, which lend a frostiness of appearance. Flowers are a clear azure blue, with prominent black anthers in a central cone. The little ring of blue petals can be slipped away and

used to garnish salad or fruit drinks – or even strung together as necklaces to amuse little girls. They may also be candied. A fresh cucumber-like fragrance is emitted from the whole plant, and it can be used to flavour cooling drinks or the leaves can be chopped and added to salads. Parkinson recommends the borage to expel pensiveness and melancholy.

Select a sunny spot or one that at least gets a good deal of sunshine during the day and where there is a well drained soil. Seed can be sown from April to July, although it will seed itself quite satisfactorily after the first season in the garden.

Brooklime *Veronica beccabunga* (Scrophulariaceae) Perennial
Water pimpernel, becky leaves, horse cress

The soft thick leaves of brooklime are generally found growing together with watercress and the two may be eaten together. Brooklime is palatable only when young but its sprawling stems with flat rounded leaves are studded along their length with tiny pale blue flowers in May and June. The entire plant shines and is quite decorative for a boggy area, stream bank or even a tiny damp herb garden made in a container. The juice, together with that of scurvy grass (*Cochlearia officinalis*) and Seville oranges, combined to form the 'spring juices' formerly valued as a remedy for scurvy. An effective diuretic, brooklime was formerly used in the treatment of gout and dropsy.

Button snakeroot *Liatris spicata* (Compositae) Perennial
Devil's bite, gay's feather

Handsome upstanding flower spikes in August commend this medicinal species as a garden plant. It flourishes in the herb garden at Acorn Bank, Cumbria (National Trust). The flowers are a rich crimson-purple and the leaves spatulate, but it is for the tuberous root that it is grown. The flavour is bitter and smells of turpentine and its main value is as a diuretic.

Camphor plant *Balsamita vulgaris* (Compositae) Perennial

This is not the camphor of commerce (that is *Cinnamomum camphora*) but a herbaceous perennial bearing white, rather flimsy, daisy-like flowers in June and July. Given a dry sheltered position, with its striking leaves it will look well at the middle or back of the border. It has a tendency to lean on its neighbours, but twiggy pea sticks pushed in early in the season will support it adequately. The foliage alone merits its inclusion in any garden, for it is glaucous, grey-green, smooth, cool to the touch and highly aromatic of camphor when bruised. Add a leaf or two to pot-pourri because they retain their fragrance well on drying. When dried and crushed, the leaves will act as a moth deterrent for blanket cupboards.

Caraway *Carum carvi* (Umbelliferae)   Biennial
Caraway, cultivated for its aromatic seed, is a good plant for a moderately heavy soil where there is some shade. The foliage is feathery and the young leaves have a mild parsley-like flavour, not at all like that of the seed. It can be chopped and added to soups and salads or used whole for garnishing. The flowers are tiny and white, appearing in July and August, and are followed by the familiar black seed. Once the seeds ripen, the heads need to be cut and the seeds allowed to fall naturally, when fully ripe, on to a sheet of paper. They are used for flavouring confectionery and liqueurs. Harvest the flower stalks and leave the plants until a week or two later. They can then be harvested for their carrot-like root, which may be used as a vegetable.

Catmint *Nepeta cataria* (Labiatae)   Perennial
Catnep, catnip
The true medicinal catnep has whitish or pale mauve flowers from June to September and small downy foliage. Strictly it is a perennial but so short-lived that it invariably behaves as a biennial. On the whole it is an unassuming plant but useful for its mint-scented leaves, which can be used to make catnip tea. Before the introduction of tea this was a household beverage.
Closely associated, and planted in many herb gardens for its deep blue-grey overall effect, is catmint, *Nepeta* x *faassenii*. Less refined in flavour, the leaves do not have the clean crisp aroma of the true catnep. Both plants hold a fascination for cats and their attention can prevent plants from forming a good shape. There is an old garden saying about these plants:
If you set it, cats will eat it,
If you sow it, the cats don't know it.
Only when it has been bruised and the aroma released do cats take notice of it, so transplanted divisions attract most attention.

Chamomile *Anthemis nobilis,* Syn. *Chamomilla nobilis* (Compositae)   Perennial.
Chamomile is a ragged, creamy-flowered little plant that sends out running shoots around itself. The double-flowered form is the one to cultivate in the herb garden, to provide dried flowerheads for chamomile tea. Four young fresh flowers or four to six dried ones can be infused to make a cupful of tea. The flowers should be gathered fresh before the petals turn brown at the back. 'Treneague' is the form to plant to make a chamomile lawn or bank, or the one to plant among paving stones, where it can be trodden upon to give off its sweet fragrance. It is a non-flowering form. The shoots quickly run about, forming a good mat-like growth of fruity fragrance, especially noticeable in warmer weather after a shower. Sandy loam provides the best medium for its roots and it likes good drainage and some sunshine.

A close relative, German chamomile (*Matricaria chamomilla*), is used in homeopathic medicine. In general appearance it is more weedy, with chalk-white single flowers with pronounced yellow centres.

Chervil *Anthriscus cerefolium* (Umbelliferae)   Annual

Chervil is cultivated chiefly for its pungent lacy foliage which strongly resembles the common cow parsley in appearance. At its best when young, the foliage is added to soups, sauces or egg dishes to impart its distinctive parsley-anise flavour. It is an ingredient of *fines herbes* and used habitually in French cooking, either dried or fresh, when it is chopped or used as a tasty garnish.

Sow a pinch of seed at regular intervals from spring to autumn to maintain a continuous supply of young leaves, because only these are used. Winter plants can be had by growing a plant or two in pots or boxes in a cool greenhouse. It seems to be rather particular about soil and likes a medium loam which is unlikely to dry out during the summer. Dappled shade suits it best.

Chicory *Cichorium intybus* (Compositae)   Perennial

The exquisite china-blue daisy flowers of the chicory are studded along the stem but have only the briefest of lives. Fresh flowers appear daily and the plants remain in bloom from July to September. In chalky districts such as the Chilterns these blue flowers are a feature of the hedgerows. The foliage resembles that of the dandelion in shape and the young leaves may be chopped for use, but later they become unacceptably bitter in flavour. They can be blanched for salads by covering the plant crowns early in the year with rhubarb forcing pots or old buckets.

Horticultural varieties are grown because the wild plant is exceedingly bitter in flavour, and the whole family is variable. Several are blanched. Most are of ancient cultivation for both culinary and medicinal use.

The ground root of Brunswick or Magdaberg chicory is used commercially as an adulterant in coffee.

Chives *Allium schoenoprasum* (Liliaceae)   Perennial

Chives have hollow grass-like leaves and form clumps, making them particularly good as edging plants. The most refined member of the onion family, they provide a clean, sharp but mild flavour, and the dainty leaves when chopped make an excellent garnish. There is a larger form, usually known as giant chives, with a somewhat stronger flavour.

The true chives like sandy to medium loam but they tolerate chalk and like a spot where there is some shade in the course of the day. Sow seed in spring and use the fresh foliage throughout the season from April to September. No plant should be stripped of all it its foliage unless it is to be discarded. Where good quality foliage is required, the rose pink or purple flowers should be prevented from blooming, but the herb garden is then deprived of one of its most attractive flowers. Use the little leaves to decorate salads or a platter of cheese or sandwiches, or float them in consommé.

Christmas rose *Helleborus niger* (Ranunculaceae)   Perennial

Like many healing herbs taken in small measured doses, the Christmas rose is valued in both orthodox and homeopathic medicine, although it is poisonous, or at least highly toxic. A more pure and innocent-looking flower could not be found, braving the inclement weather in the winter garden. All parts of the plant are poisonous, as are the other hellebores native to Britain. They were all used by medieval herbalists as strong purgatives and local anaesthetics. The hellebore was one of the truly 'knockout' drugs that used to be soaked into a vinegar or wine sponge to administer to patients before major surgery such as the amputation of a limb.

In the garden it loves a moisture-retentive loam and, once established, likes to be left undisturbed. The dark green seven or nine fingered leaves make no great show during the summer, but in the winter the plant attracts a great deal of attention and it has increased in popularity as a decorative Christmas emblem.

Coltsfoot *Tussilago farfara* (Compositae)   Perennial
Coughwort, horsehoof

Coltsfoot is not a plant to introduce into the garden except in waste corners or where it can be strictly controlled by sinking an old dustbin or bucket to restrict the wandering roots. But in representative collections of medicinal plants it adds gay yellow flowers, with stems encased in purplish grey bracts, early in the year before most other plants come into flower. It is not encountered in hedge bottoms and on railway banks as often as it used to be. In bud the flowers are upturned, then hang their heads with a seemingly half-open flower, only to stand upright again as they fade. They like a dampish soil.

Felted leaves follow after the flowers have faded. They are rounded and deeply cordate at the base, on a furrowed stalk. They can be collected and dried for inclusion in herbal tobacco or burned along with the roots to relieve obstinate coughs.

Comfrey *Symphytum officinale* (Boraginaceae)   Perennial
Knitbone, consound, boneset

A rough hairy plant, erect in habit, comfrey has drooping flowers, bell-like in little groups, blue, pink, cream or white. The leaves are rather unpleasant to handle, rough and clammy, but if collected before the plant flowers they may be used as a poultice or compress for sprains or to make an infusion to bathe painful joints. The pounded root forms a mucilaginous mass which hardens upon drying and was therefore used in the past to soak bandages to bind broken bones, acting as a plaster – hence the vernacular name of boneset.

A plant of dampish soils or waste ground and riverbanks, comfrey when cultivated needs soil that retains some moisture in summer in either half-shade or sunshine. Propagation is by division of roots in spring or autumn.

Two other species are cultivated: blue comfrey, *Symphytum caucasicum,* and Russian comfrey, *Symphytum peregrinum.* The latter seems to enjoy bursts of popularity as quickly maturing compost material for the organic gardening enthusiast and is a fodder plant. The blue or Caucasian comfrey is a smaller plant, with delightful deep blue flowers in April and May. Although it is a wanderer, it is useful for underplanting shrubs, provided the soil there is not too parched. Propagation is by division of the fleshy roots or from root cuttings taken in November.

Coriander *Coriandrum sativum* (Umbelliferae)　　　　　Annual
The round beige seeds or fruits of coriander are familiarly recognised as a flavouring for pickles and curries. Their aroma is pleasant but before ripening the entire plant is distinctly odorous. Once the fragrance develops in August and September, the seed should be collected, or the whole plant harvested and dried so that the seed will fall naturally.

In European cooking the fresh foliage has no place, but the increased interest in oriental dishes is bringing it into use, in spite of its rather stale aroma. Sow the seed in spring, in almost any soil, in an open sunny situation along a shallow drill, thinning later. The whole plant is dainty in appearance, the lower leaves fan-like, the upper ones filigree, and the tiny flowers in July are mauve.

Corn salad *Valerianella olitoria* (Valerianaceae)　　　　Annual
Lamb's lettuce, white pot herb
Though strictly a biennial plant, corn salad comes to maturity so quickly that it is grown as an annual. It is perfectly hardy and makes a good salad plant for intercropping in summer although germination is often slow during warm weather. Cover the beds with wet newspaper to hasten the process. Apart from summer crops, a succession can be had by sowing in the autumn and overwintering under cloches for an early spring supply of soft green leaves and a richer crop. Gerard said of this little herb: 'We know the Lamb's Lettuce as Loblollie; and it serves in winter as a salad herb among others none the worst'. The flowers are minute, pale lilac green and insignificant, but it is advisable to use the plants before they appear. The younger the leaves, the more refined the flavour, although some people find it insipid.

Cotton lavender *see* Lavender cotton

Cumin *Cuminum cyminum* (Umbelliferae)   Annual
Chinese parsley
   The seed is the part used, when ground, for flavouring curries
and pickles. It is a typical and habitual ingredient of Indian
curries and many other eastern dishes.
   Sow the seed in early April, to get a good start to the season's
growth, for cumin matures slowly and the seed needs to be ripe by
the middle of August. Sow in well drained soil in a sunny
protected spot where the plant's lolling habit is not going to
offend. The foliage is delicate, and the entire plant lacking in
substance so that it sprawls about. Small flowers bloom in high
summer – mauve, pink and white – followed by round seeds.
When chopped as flavouring or garnish, the foliage earns the
name of Chinese parsley, for it is a typical ingredient of Chinese
cooking.

Curry plant *Helichrysum serotinum* (Compositae)   Perennial
   A curry-like aroma pervades the air around this sub-shrub,
especially strong in warm moist weather. In the aromatic garden it
can be excessive and can easily overpower a sweeter or more
delicate fragrance. As a garden plant its chief attribute is the
tinsel-like silver-white foliage, which sparkles, especially after a
shower of rain.
   Its strong aroma perhaps suggests its use as a flavouring, but it
should not be used in this way. (It has been known to cause
vomiting.) It is generally considered to be doubtfully hardy in
many districts and its real value as a garden plant is its decorative
appearance. In winter the foliage is less silver and rather more
turquoise grey. Rusty metallic yellow flowers appear in June and
July. Propagation is from summer cuttings.

Dandelion *Taraxacum officinale* (Compositae)   Perennial
   The much abused dandelion, which if it were a rare plant would
probably be a prized garden treasure, needs no description.
Flower stalks need to be removed if the leaves are cultivated as
salad, and the early young leaves are less bitter and far superior in
texture for eating fresh. Leaves can be blanched early in the year
by covering the crowns with upturned flower pots, plastic buckets
or black polythene hoods. The winter foliage can be cooked like
spinach and seems to be preferable when mixed with sorrel,
though it then forms a strong diuretic. Crowns can be lifted and
forced during the winter to produce soft green succulent growth.
Some continental named varieties are occasionally available.
   The flat tufted yellow flowers, always so prolific in the wild,
make a good wine, and the leaves and roots are used to lend a

bitterness to herb beers.

The roots are ground and used as a caffeine-free coffee, and they are often considered to be a sedative. Lift the roots at the end of the season, scrub and dry, before grinding for coffee.

Dill *Anethum graveolens* (Umbelliferae)   Annual

Dill water was a remedy for restive infants in the early part of the twentieth century and dill is still the sweet tasting content of the proprietary gripe water.

In the kitchen its main use is in dill vinegar, which is made by macerating half a cup of dill seed in a quart (1.13 litres) of malt vinegar for three or four hours, then straining off the liquor for storage. In pickled cucumbers, a sprig of the whole plant with half-ripe seed is often an ingredient and gives a soured flavour.

Sow the seed in shallow drills in March or April, in a well drained soil and sunny position, thinning later. The filmy foliage may be collected from about six to eight weeks after sowing, to flavour fish dishes or to sprinkle on potatoes as is habitual in Poland and Czechoslovakia. The flavour is lighter than that of the seed, so sprigs of foliage are always added fresh after cooking.

The tiny yellow flowers in July and August add little to the appearance of the herb garden but then, as the round seeds form, the whole flowerheads make an effective display.

Elder *Sambucus nigra* (Caprifoliaceae)   Shrub
Elderberry

Elder grows easily from cuttings and is a rampant grower, feeding grossly and demanding light and space wherever it is introduced. For garden effect choose the golden-leaved form 'Aurea', whose foliage deepens as the season progresses, or, better still for decorative effect, *Sambucus racemosa* 'Plumosa Aurea' – the red-berried elder. This form has beautifully slashed golden leaves and creamy yellow flowerheads and is far more garden-worthy than *Sambucus nigra*.

The berries of both are edible and are used popularly for winemaking or they can be dried and added to confectionery like small currants. When the luscious black berries of the common elder are sprinkled into stewed apple as it cooks or added to apple pie, they lend an attractive pink colour. Alternatively, when the flowers are added to cooked apple, pear or gooseberry, they impart a muscatel flavour. Do not eat the berries raw, for their purgative effect is fierce, but when cooked they are more acceptable and can be added to jams, jellies and syrups. Fresh berries can be stored in the freezer.

Countless old recipes exist, suggesting delightful uses to which the plant can be put. Elderflower fritters, using a light batter, sprinkled with sugar make a delicious and unusual dessert. An old recipe for 'sambocade' uses elderflowers combined with curd cheese and egg white in a tart. Elderflower tea has a tranquillising action and soothes headaches and throat infections, although it is the berries that are mainly employed medicinally in the treatment of sore throats and coughs. Hot elderberry juice is a good household remedy for colds and influenza.

One of the best cosmetic herbs, elderflowers have for centuries been used to cure sunburn and remove freckles and coax wrinkles away. Elderflower water is an excellent skin cleanser.

Elecampane *Inula helenium* (Compositae)   Perennial
Scabwort, horseheal, velvet dock

A large handsome perennial, elecampane revels in moisture-retentive, good rich soil, where a stout clump can form. Bright yellow, rather shaggy daisy-like flowers bloom in midsummer, the petals becoming rather spiky and floppy as the flower matures. Grown for its aromatic root since Roman times, it is a good plant to introduce into the decorative herb garden because the clumps form well and establish quickly and it towers above most of the gentler herbs.

A pungent oil renders the roots astringent and strongly antiseptic, so that it has been used both for infected throats as candied lozenges and as an aid to digestion. Formerly the lozenges were coloured with cochineal and sold as a sweetmeat considered to be a treatment for bronchial and asthmatic attacks.

The vernacular names scabwort and horseheal denote its use as a veterinary treatment for the skin eruptions of farm animals. A strong diffusion of the leaves or a decoction of the root is needed, and it has been reported as being efficacious in cases of acne in adolescents.

Propagation is by division of a root clump in autumn, or by spring-sown seed. If the foliage is to be used it is best gathered young, but, to be valuable, the roots must be left to mature fully before being lifted at the end of the season, after the flowers have faded.

Evening primrose *Oenothera biennis* (Onagraceae)   Biennial
Evening star, tree primrose

The evening primrose grows in dry waste places and in the garden likes best a well drained light position, although it is not too selective of soil. Its main attribute is the sweet perfume in the evenings from the flimsy pale yellow flowers. The flowering period is long, extending throughout June, July and August and often into September. As the season progresses the flowers seem to stay open more during the day, but their evening habit of advertising their presence is to attract the insects that are on the wing during the twilight hours, for pollination.

A strong tap root is formed quickly, so care needs to be taken even when transplanting seedlings. During the second season the leaves and the bark of the stem are effective in the treatment of gastro-intestinal disorders, and there are reports of success in the treatment of whooping cough. Harvest and dry the whole plant in the summer of the second year. The mature root may be used as a vegetable like parsnip, and scientists are investigating it as a possible cure for multiple sclerosis.

In a decorative herb border, there are other species of *Oenothera* that can be introduced. Most are either biennial or monocarpic and so are not long-lived. A few species are true perennials, and these are the ones that keep their flowers open through the day, but many of them lack fragrance.

Fennel *Foeniculum vulgare* (Umbelliferae)   Perennial

A tall growing, superbly graceful plant, ideal for the back of the herb border, fennel is easily recognised by its long finely cut soft foliage. The stems are firmly upstanding and the foliage showers around it, topped by small yellow flowers from July to September. A bronze-leaved variety, often sold as black fennel, is particularly attractive.

Leaves and stems can be picked fresh throughout the summer and impart an anise-like flavour to salads or fish dishes. The foliage does not dry well, but the young shoots may be dried and stored for winter flavouring. The seed is aromatic, slightly bitter, with a less sweet anise flavour than the foliage, and is used to garnish bread and cakes. Where the flavour is enjoyed, there is a variety of ways in which it can be introduced: chopped foliage in salads or yoghurt, for example. Or, simply by baking bread on a bed of fennel stalks, a subtlety of flavour is imparted.

Sow the seed at stations along a drill in April and thin out subsequently to about 2 feet (610 mm) apart to allow the plants to spread. Alternatively, sow *in situ* in the border to form groups, allowing a reasonable distance between plants.

An annual fennel, grown for its bulbous stem-leaf base, is Florence fennel or finnochio (*Foeniculum vulgare* var *dulce,* sometimes listed as *Foeniculum dulce*). Used as a vegetable, served with a white or cheese sauce it is delicious. Seed ought not to be sown until the soil has warmed up well, or it can be started indoors or under glass and the seedlings planted out later. It is the bulbous base that is eaten late in the summer or early autumn, and it does well only in warm summers.

Fenugreek *Trigonella foenum-graecum* (Leguminosae)   Annual
Greek hayseed

A tender plant from the Mediterranean regions, fenugreek is now increasingly cultivated in gardens but is only successful in warm summers. Typical of its family, the pea flowers are creamy white and the leaves trifoliate, soft and with a sheen.

It is known best as a spicy ingredient of curry powder or when roasted as a coffee substitute. The flavour is warm and pungent. The name Greek hayseed alludes to its cultivation as a fodder plant and as a scented constituent of inferior or damaged hay mixtures. The seed adds a flavour to the foliage which cattle are said to like. It is a common ingredient of veterinary conditioning powders. The seed is aromatic and can be eaten when sprouted as a tasty salad ingredient, the flavour emanating from the seeds themselves. The soaked seed takes on a maple syrup flavour, which enhances confectionery.

Feverfew *Chrysanthemum parthenium* (Compositae)   Perennial
Featherfew, featherfoil

Feverfew is an old cottage garden plant, naturalised in many localities, and at its best where it has seeded itself. It will select gravel drive edges, old walls or roughly paved areas and will lend an air of informality to the site. Introduce it into any dry sunny corner of the garden by seed sown in spring or autumn, or by root division, or even from summer cuttings. It makes a pretty edging to beds and is an attractive plant to use to outline flower beds or beds in the general herb garden. Strictly it is a perennial, though rather short-lived, but it seeds itself so freely that it is ever present.

Its aromatic yellowish green leaves are strongly reminiscent of those of the chrysanthemum. It has ribbed stems and a profusion of small daisy-like white flowers with yellow centres, from midsummer onwards.

An infusion of feverfew, like so many cottage herbs, used to be employed as a tonic or sedative, but it is not much used today. The dried foliage acts as a moth deterrent or, when used fresh, relieves insect bites.

Foxglove *Digitalis purpurea* (Scrophulariaceae)   Biennial
Fairy thimbles

The drug digitalis is obtained from the soft green leaves of the common foxglove and, although much is imported today, one or two of the larger manufacturing chemists have their own digitalis farms in England. The plant is poisonous.

Foxgloves are a must for the decorative herb garden or representative collection of medicinal plants. The common purple foxglove likes cool shade and while it is quite happy on light soils it needs a cool root run with some compost or moisture-retentive material incorporated. Self-sown seedlings thrive best and, while they are true biennial plants, a late formed rosette may persist for the whole of the second year and flower only the following season. They should be propagated from seed sown in May or June where they are expected to flower. Plant them at the middle to the back of the border or scatter in dappled shade beneath overhanging trees.

Often their spire form is better appreciated when they can be seen against a green or darkened background. The foliage is tongue-shaped, dark green, deeply veined and soft, but the plant's beauty lies in the one-sided flower spire with dangling purplish red bells, spotted within. These have earned several descriptive country names for the plant: fairy cap, fairy glove, lady's thimble, witch's thimble, dead man's bellows, dragon's mouth or, simply, cottagers — because they belong to the poor people.

Garlic *Allium sativum* (Liliaceae)   Perennial

Garlic is often associated with highly flavoured cooked meats, and the aroma is far too strong and sulphurous for some palates. But it is used increasingly in sophisticated culinary practices, adding a subtlety of flavour which no other plant imparts. Medicinally, its use is cleansing to the blood and it is of benefit to many catarrh sufferers.

Garlic offsets need to be planted in September to allow them to establish before the winter, for the best results; or a start can be made as soon as possible in February or March so that a long growing season can be allowed, but so often a cold or wet spring leads to poor crops of garlic. Break up the bulb into individual cloves, and handle them carefully to avoid bruising. Push them upright into the soil just below the surface. They need to be planted in short rows or planted in a block over a small area. Prevent the white flowers from blooming by nipping them out, so that the bulbs will mature in summer. The top growth will begin to turn colour when they are ripe.

A small quantity of garlic added to meat dishes, stews or cooked meats will heighten any existing flavour, and a fresh broken clove rubbed round a salad bowl will improve any green salad enormously. If too much is eaten, so that the aroma hangs on the breath, relieve it by chewing parsley.

Gentian *Gentiana lutea* (Gentianaceae)   Perennial
Bitterwort

The yellow gentian was the first of its genus to be introduced into cultivation in Britain, and Gerard grew it in his garden, calling it felwort. Gentian bitters are extracted from the enormous spongy root, which plunges down into the soil as much as a yard. In the Alps, where its statuesque growth is a feature of low meadow slopes, the roots are lifted in autumn, when they are richest in gentianin, and made into gentian brandy. The bitterness of the root makes it one of the most effective tonics.

As a garden plant, in a representative medicinal collection, it takes a while to establish itself but can live for a couple of generations where it is happy. The yellow star-like flowers are clustered around the stem at intervals, in July and August, held by important-looking cup-shaped leaves, which in pairs enfold the flowers. Propagation is by seed, but the ensuing seedlings need to be transplanted with considerable care, so that the brittle young roots are not damaged.

Germander *Teucrium chamaedrys* (Labiateae)   Perennial
Wall germander

Formerly much cultivated for its medicinal properties, germander's claim to inclusion in the herb garden nowadays is as a substantial edging plant. It is one of the aromatic plants that was used to outline the Tudor knot garden and can be clipped to retain a formal shape.

Its principal use was in the treatment of flatulence, to aid digestion and as a flavouring for liqueurs and tonic wines. It imparts a bitter clean flavour.

The small dark green leaves are shaped like those of the oak. Tiny rosy flowers appear in June and July, but the foliage is the main attribute.

Propagated by seed sown in the spring or from summer cuttings, it soon forms a good bushy little plant which is perfectly hardy in spite of its southern European origins. Almost any soil supports it, and it is tolerant of some light shade.

Goat's rue *Galega officinalis* (Leguminosae)   Perennial

This pretty light-hearted plant always adds a decorative touch to the herb garden. The foliage is soft and typical of the family and the flowers are carried in short spikes of sweet-pea shaped blooms of mauve and blue (sometimes white) in June and July. Its rather untidy habit suggests that it ought to be put at the back of the border where it can be concealed after flowering. Good twiggy pea sticks provide suitable stakes, which it will obliterate as the season proceeds.

It is from the dried flowering shoots that a tisane is made for diabetes, especially of the elderly. Ancient lore credits it as a stimulant to lactation and as a plant fed to animals for this purpose. Modern herbals seem to regard this action as doubtful, but it is an allusion to this property that has given it its common name of goat's rue, the foliage being not dissimilar to that of rue.

Good King Henry *Chenopodium bonus henricus*
(Chenopodiaceae)   Perennial
Goosefoot, mercury, allgood

In much the same way that spinach is used today, Good King Henry was formerly used as a vegetable. Its renewed appearance in the kitchen garden is apparent, and the soft arrow-shaped leaves, when boiled and flavoured with a sprinkling of lemon juice, make a good green-leaf vegetable. The green young shoots may be peeled, boiled and used in the same way as asparagus. It is considered to be a highly nutritious vegetable.

Cultivate it on well worked loamy soil and it will continue to produce for a number of years. Sow seed in drills in April, thinning subsequently, and allow the plants to establish themselves during the first year, cutting only in subsequent years. Always leave enough foliage on the plant to maintain it in health. Established plants can be divided in April.

The vernacular name smearwort refers to its use as an ingredient of an ointment to cleanse chronic skin eruptions.

Henbane *Hyoscyamus niger* (Solanaceae)   Annual or biennial
Henbell, belene

In appearance the henbane seems to be an evil plant, and it was one of those that used to be closely associated with madness and delirium, part of the witches' brew, full of magical powers and highly poisonous. It is little wonder that in unskilled hands it had drastic effects. To add to the mysterious air, both annual and biennial seedlings can come from seed from the same capsule. Its slightly foetid smell, coming from the pale, prickly and somewhat sticky leaves does not endear it. The flowers appear to be mauve but are really cream so thickly pencilled with purple lines that only on close inspection is their beauty seen. The green-brown seed capsules late in the season resemble decayed human teeth and under the doctrine of signatures were interpreted as signifying that the plant should be used in the relief of toothache. This is the plant, used in extract, that Dr Crippen employed in murdering his wife.

Horehound *Marrubium vulgare* (Labiatae)   Perennial
Hoarhound

The white horehound, so called because the silky hairs that adorn the plant give it a frosty appearance, has a strong smell and the extract of the leaves is extremely bitter in flavour. The leaves are much wrinkled and dusty or hairy in appearance, and the stems also are felted with hairs. A candy is made for the alleviation of coughs by boiling down the washed herbs until the juice is extracted or by using an electrical juice extractor and boiling the resultant liquid with sugar until it is thick enough to set when cooled. The quantities necessary are at least 1 pound (0.45 kg) of sugar to 1 pint (0.57 litres) of liquid. Gather the herb just before flowering for it to be most effective.

A hardy native plant, not much seen growing in the wild these days, it needs a drying, poor soil to flourish in the garden. Propagation is by division in spring and often it does not flower the summer after being divided.

The offensive smell of black horehound (*Ballota nigra*) keeps it from being much cultivated. It has rose-purple flowers and less hairy leaves than the white horehound.

Horseradish *Armoracia rusticana* (Cruciferae)   Perennial

A coarse-growing perennial whose natural home is eastern Europe, horseradish is grown for its tapering fleshy root, which provides the condiment. The taste is biting, mustard-like and very penetrating, only at its best when the root has been grated or thinly sliced. When it is unbroken it is inodorous and so can be stored easily for quite a long period. Formerly it was used as a cosmetic, considered to be effective in clearing freckles and maintaining a clear complexion. It is also used in the same way as a mustard plaster, to give relief to aching joints.

On account of its deeply thrusting root, the horseradish requires a deeply worked soil and is usually raised from root cuttings or pieces of root planted out in February or March. Some roots can be left in the ground at the end of the growing season to provide pieces for the following spring. Others can be stored and used for the kitchen. Renew the bed of horseradish about every third year.

Hound's tongue *Cynoglossum officinale* (Boraginaceae) Perennial
Gipsyflower, scaldhead, rosenoble

Hound's tongue is a stout plant, tough of texture, with leaves resembling the shape and roughness of a dog's tongue. Gerard said also: 'It will tye the tongues of Houndes so that they shall not bark at you, if it be laid under the bottom of your feet'. Previous to Gerard, it had been administered in the belief that it could cure stuttering. When the doctrine of signatures was a prevalent belief, this resemblance led to the use of the plant in the treatment of dog bite.

Although it is a British native plant it is not commonly found in the wild state. But seed is available and as a garden plant it thrives best on gravel or sandy soil and it tolerates both drought and exposure without ill effects, making a suitable plant for a seaside herb garden. The little bur-like seeds are covered with tiny hooked spines and ought to be sown in August.

The name scaldhead is a combination of two uses to which an impregnated grease or oil of hound's tongue was formerly put: firstly as an application to scalds, and secondly to rub over a bald head in the firm belief that hair would be restored.

Houseleek *Sempervivum tectorum* (Crassulaceae)   Perennial
Thunder plant, Jupiter's beard, jubarb
The bareness of its habitat and its undemanding nature make
the houseleek an easy plant to cultivate. Sometimes it can appear
slow to establish. Planting the tiny offsets at almost any time of
the year between paving stones or in crannies or around the edges
of a trough – anywhere where a porous environment encourages
the roots to form – is sufficient to start a colony. The
conglomerate growth is always cool to the touch: each wedge-
shaped leaf is a living reservoir, enabling the plant to survive in
seemingly adverse conditions.
Herbalists regard it as one of the safest remedies for
inflammation and swelling, and a portion of bruised leaf is
recommended to be rubbed over the affected part. A fresh leaf
crushed above the eye so as to exude the juice directly in was
reputed to dispel styes and clear inflammation but it is always
important to seek advice before self-treatment for the eyes.
The English name of thunder plant is reminiscent of a belief,
widespread in Europe in the dark ages, that to have houseleek
growing on a roof was a charm against being struck by lightning.
More practically, the name *Sempervivum tectorum* means 'ever
living plant of the roof' and suggests that it was mainly
established there to retain the roofing material.

Hyssop *Hyssopus officinalis* (Labiatae)   Perennial
An aromatic shrubby little evergreen with tiny blue flowers
from June to September and small leaves, hyssop is attractively
employed as an edging plant in the herb garden. It is often over-
looked: its appearance is unassuming but its aroma is pungent
and distinctive. The foliage needs to be rubbed to release it, but
fresh leaves sprinkled into soups and stews add piquancy.
Both flowers and leaves dry well and are good ingredients for
pot-pourri as they retain their aroma. If the flowers are gathered
as they reach maturity and dried, they can be used to make an
infusion which, together with honey, relieves chest troubles. If the
fresh green growing tips are picked and dried in summer an
infusion made from them is useful in the treatment of catarrh.
Propagation is from spring-sown seed or from summer cuttings
taken with a heel. Hyssop prefers a light garden soil and sunny
position. Once established, the plants tolerate clipping and so
may be used as a formal edging. When they are to be used in this
way the clippings ought to be preserved and dried as a harvest, as
the plants will not tolerate a clipping *and* a harvesting.

Indian physic *Gillenia trifoliata* (Rosaceae)   Perennial
Bowman's root, gillenia
As a perennial herb indigenous to the United States, where the

American Indians and early colonists used the roots, Indian physic is an interesting plant to include in a collection of medicinal herbs. Its action is drastic (and perhaps suspect) but the root also provides a red dye.

It flourishes in the herb garden at Acorn Bank, Cumbria, and has oval veined leaves and dainty white flowers held well above them. The noteworthy characteristic of the plant is the red colouring of the stems and large calyces. It enjoys dappled shade in a slightly rich, moist loam.

Iris *see* Orris

Jacob's ladder *Polemonium caeruleum* (Polemoniaceae)
Greek valerian, charity   Perennial
The common name refers to the shape of the little leaves: it is not a valerian, but there is a slight resemblance in the leaves and cats give their attention to this plant, as they do to valerian. As late as the mid nineteenth century it was used mainly as an anti-syphilitic agent and in the treatment of rabies. It has fallen out of use medicinally but appears to be being reintroduced into medicinal herb collections.

The helmet-shaped flowers are of an intense blue in midsummer, and there is a white-flowered form. A variegated-leaved form is also recorded but I have not seen it. Propagation is from division of the creeping rootstock in spring or autumn, but the plants seed themselves so easily that there is usually a plentiful supply of young plants. They like any good garden soil, provided that there is no surface moisture.

Juniper *Juniperus communis* (Coniferae)   Perennial
The ripe berries of the common juniper vary considerably in flavour according to where the shrubs grow, and it is apparent that some good sun baking is necessary to heighten and refine the flavour. Berries ought to be blue and sweet and resinous. Their flavour goes well in marinades, for rich meats such as venison and pork, and they are used in the making of sauerkraut. They need to be crushed in a mortar to release the full flavour. They are known best, perhaps, as a flavouring for gin and steinhager, when oil of juniper is usually used.

The shrub is difficult to buy, and there appears to be a dearth in garden centres and nurseries. But it can, with patience, be propagated from cuttings or from seed, which takes a long time to germinate. It is best to sow it in a seed pan and forget about it.

Lavender *Lavandula spica* (Labiatae)   Perennial
Lavender, the most readily recognised herb, can be included on two counts: for its decorative usefulness as a garden plant, and

for its use in perfumery. The essential oil when extracted is known as oil of lavender and the quality depends as much upon climate as on the strain of the plant. Oil produced in England is some of the finest in the world, certainly richer than that produced in Mediterranean regions.

The gardener may be bewildered by the various kinds of lavender, but two main types are grown in Britain, the dwarf and standard kinds. The standard lavenders include varieties such as 'Grappenhall', and the various forms include Old English or Mitcham lavender, Seal lavender, Dutch lavender and grey hedge lavender. All have grey-green foliage and purple flower spikes and attain more than 2 feet (610 mm) in height.

The dwarf and semi-dwarf lavenders have a more compact habit, especially perhaps the Hidcote varieties like 'Hidcote Purple'. The plants also have grey-green leaves but are never more than 2 feet (610 mm) in height and are pricked with flower spikes like great pincushions. The flowers vary from blue-mauve in 'Folgate Blue' to deep purple in 'Munstead Dwarf'.

All lavenders prefer well drained soil with a lime content and like to be firmly planted. Where lavender is grown for garden effect it is advisable to take a batch of cuttings each year to maintain a regular supply of young plants for replacements. The useful decorative effect of many lavender plants diminishes after five or six years and time spent on trying to refurbish them is better spent in grubbing them up and replacing with young plants. A leggy bush, bare at the base, is ugly and frequently tends to lean to one side. Propagation is from heeled cuttings taken in August and early September and rooted in sandy compost or a proprietary cutting compost.

The immense popularity of lavender in both the herb garden and the flower garden is out of all proportion to its usefulness. It is grown only for its dryish flower spikes, useful for decoration and sweet-smelling conceits such as lavender bags. The foliage, as well as the flowers, is a good ingredient of pot-pourri.

Lavender bags. Both flowers and leaves can be used in pot-pourri and because the flowers hold their perfume so well on drying they are put into sachets. For this, the flower spikes are cut while in fat bud, before the petals unfurl, and are dried by spreading out the stems on paper or cloth in a warm room, garden shed or airing cupboard. Sunshine will bleach the colour, so shade the flowers while they are drying, and once the buds can be rubbed free of the stems they are ready for use. In a warm room this will take three to four weeks, less in a warm cupboard. Lavender is a powerful sternutatory, so a smog mask or even a simple respirator needs to be worn when rubbing the flowers – and protect domestic animals from the dust. The rubbed-off flowers are sieved to separate them from dust and bracts and are then ready for packing into sachets or small bags.

Lavender cotton *Santolina* species (Compositae) Perennial
Santolina, cotton lavender

Given full sun in a well drained spot, the santolinas are among the best sub-shrubs with aromatic foliage. They are grown mainly for the grey-white foliage, which persists throughout the year, and benefit from being close-clipped in spring to encourage new growth and prevent them from becoming leggy and developing bare patches in the centre. Propagation is by cuttings taken in the summer. *Santolina chamaecyparissus* (Syn. *Santolina incana*) has thread-like foliage, resembling silver coral, and forms a cushion of growth which is decorated in July and August with yellow bobble flowers. The foliage is pungent and aromatic. The form *Santolina chamaecyparissus insularis,* catalogued sometimes as *Santolina neopolitana,* is slightly taller, softer and looser of habit, with feathered pungent foliage, and, catalogued as 'Sulphurea', has primrose yellow flowers set off by rather greener leaves. It is a useful plant in the decorative herb garden. Another good species to try is *Santolina virens,* with compact bushy growth of emerald green, slightly oily to the touch and highly aromatic, almost camphorous.

Lavender cotton foliage, dried well, retains its aroma and is a good insecticide to scatter in cupboards and drawers, if the smell of camphor is liked. Combine some foliage with cloves in china pomanders for the wardrobe.

Lemon balm *Melissa officinalis* (Labiatae) Perennial
Sweet balm, balm

A rounded bush-like perennial with richly aromatic bright green leaves and somewhat insignificant flowers from mid to late summer, lemon balm is a true cottage garden plant and best in that form. A variegated-leaved form *M.o.* 'variegata' is popularly cultivated but can appear somewhat messy. There is a golden-leaved form *M.o.* 'Aurea', worth growing in dappled shade to maintain the fresh butter yellow colour. The rounded leaves are deeply veined, strongly scented of lemon with a rather stale overtone, so it is important to use them when they are young before the flowering period. The leaves dry well and may be included in pot-pourri.

A tea or tisane made from the fresh or dried leaves is delicious, flavoured with a little honey. It is a favourite herb tea, recommended particularly for fevers and colds to promote perspiration and 'bring the fever out'. The leaves may also be added to salads with some restraint and used dried in stuffings. Commercially they are employed in perfumery and in flavouring liqueurs.

Give lemon balm a good garden soil, retentive of moisture, in a sunny corner, or somewhere where it at least has some neighbours, for all true cottage garden plants like a friendly environment. Propagation is best carried out by division of roots in spring or autumn.

Lemon verbena *Lippia citriodora,* Syn. *Aloysia triphylla, Lippia triphylla* (Verbenaceae)   Perennial

A tender perennial which dies down each winter and is not suitable for cultivation out of doors in elevated or cool areas, lemon verbena is also a good plant for a conservatory or garden room and may be cultivated in a pot. Its long narrow pointed leaves have the purest and most refreshing aroma of all lemon-scented plants. The flower spikes are a secondary feature of the plant.

Out of doors, tuck it into a dry and very sheltered corner, at the base of a wall where the soil is none too good, then the roots will come through most winters. My plant came through the severe winter of 1979-80 unscathed, although it broke later than usual. Use a leaf or two in pot-pourri – too much can unbalance the resultant mixture with a lemony sharpness, so definite is the scent. As with any other aromatic plant, the foliage is at its best just before the plant comes into bloom. A tisane can be made from the dried foliage, said to be helpful for snuffly noses.

Lily-of-the-valley *Convallaria majalis* (Liliaceae)   Perennial
May lily

This is a poisonous plant, but one used in the treatment of cardiac conditions in eastern Europe and considered to be very effective. It should be grown in a herb garden only as a representative plant. Its twin broad leaves appear early in spring, spearing the ground in little rolls, and unfurl to enfold a single stem of pendulous, highly fragrant white bells.

Given a dampish woodland calcareous soil, the plants will quickly form a good colony, spreading by the stoloniferous roots. Propagation is by division of clumps or by breaking off a portion from the outside of the cluster of root mass.

Cultivation in pots is straightforward; lily-of-the-valley will scent a conservatory at Easter, and by careful management plants may be had in flower until June. Plump crowns are potted up in a Number 1 potting compost and leaf mould in the autumn and kept out of doors to settle. Once indoors keep them in a dark cool place until growth is about 5 inches (127 mm) in height. Admit light and give warmth gradually until they are taken into a warm living room and watered as growth proceeds. Specially retarded crowns can be purchased for forcing in this way. If planted out in the garden after flowering they may not flower the following year, but subsequently they will recover.

Many beds of lily-of-the-valley draw attention again later in the year by their coral-red berries. Where mass planting has been undertaken the effect is good, as it is in the herb garden at Cranborne Manor, Dorset.

Lime *Tilia cordata* (Tiliaceae)   Perennial

The lime is a tree native to England and Wales, especially on limestones, and is planted in gardens and streets and in the great avenue at Hampton Court. Lime flowers have been used for generations to make a pleasant tisane and the tree has a place in European folklore medicine. At one time it seems to have been a cure-all administered for a wide range of complaints from feverish chills to chest congestion. But linden tea, as the tisane is known, is a certain remedy for headaches and for poor digestion. It carries the delicate scent of the lime flowers, a scent used in cosmetics such as soap to add a fresh sweetness.

Liquorice *Glycyrrhiza glabra* (Leguminosae)   Perennial

The liquorice root is used in medicine as a mild purgative, and supplies are usually imported. Previously it was grown commercially in some quantity in Yorkshire in the Pontefract area, but how successful the crops were is not recorded. In cold climates the roots tend to grow fibrous and woody. It is also employed in the treatment of coughs, as a flavouring for lozenges.

The plant is quite decorative and is to be seen in some of the larger herb gardens and representative collections. The flowers are typical of the pea family, pale lavender in colour, and the foliage is very soft and folds up and droops each evening.

Propagation is from root cuttings in spring, and as the plants become established it is usual to cut back the top growth to stimulate root formation. After three or four years, cutting back each year, the roots are harvested. Seed may also be sown in spring, or plants can be divided in spring or autumn.

Loosestrife *Lythrum salicaria* (Lythraceae)   Perennial
Purple loosestrife

An invaluable perennial for planting in dampish places, purple loosestrife revels in the muddy banks of streams and ponds and loves moist soils. The type is not often seen: garden cultivars are usually grown and make a brilliant addition to the herb garden. They are richer and brighter in flower and the poker-like rose-purple flower spikes are a good contrast to many of the less robust herbs. 'Prichard Variety', 'Robert', 'Firecandle' and 'Brightness' are all reliable cultivars. 'Robert' is lower growing than the remainder and is ideal for the front of the border.

Loosestrife was used formerly in tanning leather, and in dilute quantities as an eye wash. It is said to be an excellent gargle and wound cleanser with an antibacterial action. Propagation is by division of the clumps in spring, and non-flowering shoots may be used as cuttings.

Lovage *Levisticum officinale* (Umbelliferae)   Perennial
Indian dolphin

A hardy herbaceous perennial with lusciously healthy green leaves and yellowish green flowers in umbels in July and August, lovage offers a good substitute in cooking for celery, as a pot herb, adding a stronger flavour rather more nutty than that of celery. The young growth of both foliage and stems can be added to salads, with some discretion because of the potency of the flavour. Harvested in late summer, when ripe, the aromatic seed is useful to flavour bread and pastries or to sprinkle on boiled rice or boiled potato. The roots are edible but require to be stripped of their bitter skin to render them palatable.

Most soils are suitable, and lovage is shade-tolerant, provided it gets sunshine at some time of the day. Give it a moist spot if possible, with some humus-enriching material worked in well, and it will repay with good resilient stems. A handsome plant, frequently not recognised, it ought to be more widely cultivated in the herb garden for it lustrous foliage alone.

Propagation is by July sown seed, or the roots can be divided in late autumn after the top growth has died down. Attractive bronze shoots emerge in the spring.

Lungwort *Pulmonaria officinalis* (Boraginaceae)   Perennial
Jerusalem cowslip, soldiers and sailors, lung moss

Lungwort is cultivated in many gardens for its spotted foliage and its flowers, which come at the same time as primroses and change colour so that there are always pink and blue ones at the same time. Lungwort has been grown for centuries for its foliage, which contains mucilage, effective in the treatment of coughs and colds. Spring leaves can be chopped and added to salads and resemble borage in that they are of a cucumber flavour.

Choose a shaded area with good moisture-retentive soil and lungwort will be a good ground-cover plant. It forms extensive patches in woodland conditions and when the more silver-leaved species (*Pulmonaria saacharata*), sometimes called Bethlehem sage, is grown it can light up the ground beneath shrubs in a darkish corner. While this species is not strictly a herb it begs a place in the decorative herb garden.

Propagation is by division of roots in late summer after flowering. Once the flowers are over the growth tends to die down and fresh basal rosettes of leaves are formed. These are the pieces to separate. Spring division is also reliable when the ground can be worked early in the season, but many springs are either too wet or too cold for this operation to be successful in all but the milder districts. But lungwort tends to seed itself quite freely. If seedlings are not required it is advisable to remove old flowerheads.

Mace, English *Achillea decolorans* (Compositae)　　　　Perennial

The mace of commerce is derived from the dried outer seedcase of the nutmeg (*Myristica fragrans*). English mace is totally inferior, but the vernacular name simply pays homage to the fact that the flavour is hot, spicy and pungent. The plant has come to be known in some localities as the nutmeg plant. Leaves of this mace can be added to soups and stews or goulash-type dishes just to lend a dash of flavour.

The cream daisy flowers in June and July are of no special interest and the foliage is dark green and deeply divided. Mace is not often seen in cultivation but worthy of a place in the culinary herb collection. Propagation is by division in spring or autumn, and the pieces should be planted into a moderately rich soil in an open but sheltered spot. Where the soil is not sufficiently rich the foliage tends to become rather rank. It dries well and retains its pungency. The crowns may need to be protected in cold seasons or harsh areas, but by taking cuttings in July plants can be easily maintained in a frame or with some other slight protection in unfavourable areas.

Mallow *Malva sylvestris* (Malvaceae)　　　　Biennial
Cheeses

The common mallow is a wild plant in Britain and strictly a biennial although it often forms a woody base and behaves as a short-lived perennial. Mauve-pink flat-faced flowers, each petal sketched with fine lines, are tucked among the soft rounded lobed leaves. Formerly used as a mild laxative, the seed heads, known as 'cheeses' because of their shape, can be added fresh to salads.

Propagation is from seed, sown in the early summer and the straggly little mallow plants that result look best tucked among the stonework of steps or a retaining wall.

For medicinal purposes it has largely been replaced by the marsh mallow (*Althea officinalis*) with softer-textured foliage and rather pinker flowers in later summer. Tolerant of sun and wind, this mallow is a good maritime plant provided that it is growing in moisture-retentive material. Again, the flattened seed heads can be eaten fresh. The foliage is a good salad ingredient when young and fresh or a useful addition to stews or vegetable broths when older. An infusion of dried leaves is refreshing as a tea or a soothing eye bath. There is a long tradition of using marsh mallow as a soothing treatment for coughs and chest complaints in the form of a syrup. It is the roots that are used to combat inflammation of the digestive tract.

It is good plant for the back of the border in the herb garden. The flowers retain a translucent quality on drying and are said to add their rose colouring to wine. Propagation is from seed sown in spring to produce stout rich spires of flower the following season.

Marigold *Calendula officinalis* (Compositae)   Annual
Pot marigold, marygold

The golden marigold needs no introduction even to the town dweller, and it is the most reliable of summer flowering annuals. Seedsmen offer a range of forms, all of them double-flowered, in a variety of yellow and orange shades. But the true officinal plant is a small single-flowered daisy, with a single row of pale orange-yellow ray petals and sometimes with a slightly darker central zone.

The flowers and leaves of this plant, and indeed of all garden cultivars, add flavour to salads or soups. But unless the leaves are very young they are acrid and unacceptable to some palates. Flower petals make a pretty garnish to meat platters, pâté and fruit salad and add colour to curd cheese or a piquancy to yoghurt.

Numerous recipes including marigold can be discovered in old household books, and it was even believed that only to look upon marigolds strengthened the eyesight and 'withdrew evil humours out of the head'. The mucilage extracted from the whole plant has a healing action; marigold ointment was an old household remedy. A lotion made from the extraction restored the complexion, or a mixture of the extraction and cold cream made a perfect cleansing cream.

Sow the seed in spring in a sunny spot preferably in a fine loam, but the marigold is tolerant of a wide range of soils provided there is no waterlogging. For window boxes, tubs and other containers sow *in situ*. In the summer some plants will develop a fibrous base and overwinter, especially in sheltered places. Self-sown seedlings usually inhabit the garden too, once marigolds have been introduced. In dry areas autumn-sown seed provides good plants for effect as early as May the following year.

Marjoram *Origanum* species (Labiatae)   Perennial

All marjorams have a strong warm flavour in their leaves, and to some extent in the flowers. Sweet or knotted marjoram (*Origanum majorana*) is a perennial plant from the warm countries around the Mediterranean, and so in cooler climates, such as Britain's, it is usually treated as an annual. Rather rougher in flavour and much hardier, pot marjoram (*Origanum*

43

onites) is the plant more usually grown, simply because it will tolerate the dampness more easily.

Both plants produce small twiggy stems, brittle to the touch and bedecked with aromatic leaves. Pot marjoram has either white or pink flowers in midsummer; sweet marjoram always has pink flowers. Various leaf forms are to be found, some with a golden yellow splash across one corner of the leaf, others with golden leaves, and others, less aromatic, with pure gold leaves – very useful for the decorative herb garden, where they can be well used to form the edge of a bed or border.

Used as a flavouring since ancient times, the marjorams were also in demand for strewing in public places and dwellings. Flower tops can be used to decorate salads or garnish meat dishes, or they can be sprinkled into cooling drinks in summer. It is the leaves that are used mainly, in both French and English cookery, often in conjunction with thyme – which marjoram strongly resembles in flavour – as a constituent of *bouquet garni.*

Wild marjoram (*Origanum vulgare*) is known as oregano and grows wild all over Europe, including Britain. (In some countries, notably Mexico and the southern United States, oregano is a colloquial name for unrelated plants, which have a similar flavour.) It is wild marjoram, especially that of southern Europe, where the flavour is more biting than from the British plants, that gives the characteristic flavour to the Neapolitan pizza and is commonly used in the preparation of cold stuffed meats and sausages.

All the marjorams dry well for winter use, and all can be incorporated in pot-pourri – either flowers or leaves.

Propagation is from seed, sown in spring, or, for pot and wild marjoram, cuttings can be taken in early summer or the plants divided in the autumn. The wild marjoram is a more sprawling plant, which is best cut back in autumn to overwinter and form new shoots again the following spring. Marjorams all like to have plenty of sunshine and good soil; well grown plants are superior in flavour to those that are cultivated in shade or in dry soils.

Melilot *Melilotus officinalis* (Papilionaceae)   Biennial
Common melilot, hart's clover

Spikes of bright yellow pea flowers in midsummer, held in an elegant fashion on long spikes all over the bushy plant, are the chief delight of melilot. A tea made from the fresh flowers relieves indigestion and flatulence and the fresh leaves make a good poultice for aching joints. The almond-like fragrance commends the plant in the scented garden, where the bees love it. The fragrance remains on drying and, indeed, increases in the same way as that of woodruff because they both contain coumarin. This is why it has been used for generations as a fodder plant. It is now naturalised on waste land in many localities in Britain.

Propagation is from seed, and if this is sown early in the spring the plant will behave as an annual, coming into flower the same year, but if the seed is sown in high summer, melilot will overwinter and flower the following May and June.

Mignonette *Reseda odorata* (Resedaceae)   Perennial
Little darling, sweet mignonette

Strictly a perennial but usually grown as an annual, mignonette was grown much more a century ago than it is today. It atones for its somewhat insignificant flower colour with a strong musky perfume. Modern plants suffer from the loss of much of the scent through cultivation, resulting in a lack of popularity. But in Victorian times the mignonette was a pot plant *par excellence,* used for parlour, greenhouse, conservatory and window-box decoration. Beloved of bees and useful for drying to add to pot-pourri, it can be grown in any sunny corner where the soil is light and firm. Flowers are reddish green in June and July and seedsmen are now offering 'sweet' varieties claimed to be fragrant.

The upright mignonette (*Reseda alba*) is sweetly scented of almond, more strongly than any other species. The leaves are particularly deeply divided and the flower spikes of small white flowers come in June. Often the plant behaves as a biennial or, at best, a very short-lived perennial.

Mint *Mentha* species (Labiatae)   Perennial

Most people can recognise a few of the numerous species and forms of mint, which are an interesting tribe of plants, ranging from *Mentha requienii,* the smallest known plant in Britain, to *Mentha* × *villosa*, Bowles's mint, with large hairy leaves. For culinary use the true pea mint flavour is needed and this mint has it, as has the common green lamb mint, *Mentha spicata,* the commonest mint of all.

Medicinally, the peppermints are derived from *Mentha* × *piperita,* peppermint oil being used in pharmaceutical flavouring. Peppermint tea, made from either fresh or dried leaves of this mint, is ready to drink in three or four minutes after infusion, and it makes a refreshing aid to digestion.

Decorative forms of *Mentha suaveolens,* formerly *Mentha rotundifolia,* have come to be recognised as apple mint or monk's herb and have a soft green foliage marked with cream, or sometimes a whole young shoot is cream. This adds a lightening effect to the whole herb border. The scent is strongly suggestive of apples and the leaves taste good used in salads. The pineapple mint, *Mentha suaveolens* 'Variegata', has a very fruity fragrance and delightful pale green and cream leaves. The variation in the degree of mintiness makes an interesting reason for including several different mints in the herb garden. The ginger mint, *Mentha × gentilis*, is at first quite minty in aroma, but when the leaves are rubbed a distinct ginger spicy aroma is released. *Mentha × piperita citrata* seems to have a string of popular names – and catalogue names too. It is variously eau-de-cologne mint, orange mint, lemon mint or bergamot mint, and, however the fragrance strikes, it is a good addition to the herb garden.

Pennyroyal, *Mentha pulegium,* has two forms, one upright and the other creeping. Both are wild plants in the southern counties of England, and the creeping one is especially decorative when tucked among paving stones where its roots can find some moisture. Pennyroyal is pungent, like peppermint but lacking the freshness.

The kitchen garden mints are by far the most widely known and used. *Mentha spicata,* spearmint or garden mint, is most frequently encountered. The horse mint, *Mentha longifolia* (sometimes still called *Mentha sylvestris*), has similar foliage and both are distinguished from all other mints by their narrow long foliage. Mint jelly and mint vinegar, or mint sauce, are most satisfactorily made from these two. Although the connoisseur's mint for the making of mint sauce is *Mentha × villosa alopecuroides,* its hairy leaves may discourage some cooks from trying them, but once chopped the hairiness disappears.

The soft leaves of all the mints dry fairly well but need special care to maintain a good clean colour as it is so easy for them to turn black. Try not to gather too many shoots at one time so that they can be well spread out to dry and thus dry properly. All the mints can be included in pot-pourri – the fruity ones are best – or put into sachets for storing in drawers and cupboards. Then if they are crushed or rubbed occasionally the dried leaves will release their aroma afresh. All of them can be used as an infusion, sometimes sweetened with honey to taste, known as mint ale.

All mints are propagated by pulling away a rooted runner. This is a good example of what the gardener calls an Irishman's cutting. The little runners planted out soon form new roots and are off to hunt territory of their own, for the mints are all great travellers. To restrain them, it is often necessary to contain them in an old bucket or tub sunk into the ground. Alternatively, the mint bed needs to be replanted every three years or so and often mint fails to grow because no thought has been given to the location of the bed. The uninitiated gardener often believes that because a plant is commonly grown it is accommodating, and this is not always so. Remaking the mint bed disposes of the old stringy runners and overcomes the weeding problem to a considerable extent because once mint runners are established weeding is virtually impossible.

Motherwort *Leonorus cardiaca* (Labiatae)   Perennial
Once established in ordinary soil where there is good light, motherwort survives the hardest winters because of its creeping underground stems. Tall square reddish stems carry pairs of long pointed deeply veined leaves with purplish white flowers nestling in the axils. Since the seventeenth century its power as a fertility drug has been known.

Mugwort *Artemisia vulgaris* (Compositae)   Perennial
If ever a beautiful plant were dubbed with an unattractive name, it is surely this artemisia. The pretty apple green deeply segmented foliage glistens, especially after rain, and forms a rounded sub-shrub which in time becomes quite woody at the base. Strongly aromatic of sweet camphor-mint, a few leaves in the bath water will relieve tired feet.

Mullein *Verbascum thapsus* (Scrophulariaceae)   Biennial
Blanket weed, Aaron's rod, hag's taper
Mullein is a denizen of waste places, roadsides or other grassy places in Britain but has long been cultivated in cottage gardens. The unique characteristic of mullein is the rosette of large thick felt-like silver-white leaves. They diminish in size and number up the height of the stem and the tall yellow flower spike blooms in July and August. The general hairiness of the plant renders it susceptible to winter dampness and in some situations, where the drainage is poor, the leaves may need picking over or constantly brushing free of debris. Mullein seeds itself easily, so once introduced into the garden there is little need to ensure its continuance. Propagation, however, is from seed sown in summer, and the rosette will be formed the first season, the flower spike produced the second.

The leaves, collected especially in the first year, are used to make an infusion for the relief of pulmonary congestion, but the liquor needs to be meticulously strained to eliminate the hairs, which otherwise act as an irritant. The dried leaves are used as a herb tobacco. The down from the stems and leaves used to be stripped off and used as tinder and lamp wicks. The erect tall hairy stem, after dipping in tallow or suet, was used to make a torch or rush light, hence the name hag's taper.

Nasturtium *Tropaeolum majus* (Tropaeolaceae)   Annual
'Nasturtium' is a misnomer: the garden nasturtium, so easily recognised with its orange long-spurred flowers, bears the true Latin name of the watercress *(Nasturtium officinale)*. The confusion has most likely arisen because of the peppery taste of the round leaves. These round leaves, held at right angles to the stem, can best be used by rubbing a broken leaf round the salad

bowl to flavour a green salad. The seeds are sometimes included in pickles and chutneys, but this practice seems to be falling into disfavour. They are peppery in flavour.

Raise a fresh supply of plants each year, for decoration in the herb garden, or for containers such as window boxes. There are trailing kinds and dwarf forms also. The nasturtium is a useful plant giving quick results, always encouraging in children's gardens. Unfortunately it seems to attract blackfly.

Nettle *Urtica dioica* (Urticaceae)   Perennial

The nettle needs no description. It is one of the first plants children learn to recognise. The young leaves can be used in the spring as a green-leaf vegetable, known as 'nettle tops' and served like spinach, with a knob of butter or a sprinkling of caraway seed. The stinging hairs are rendered innocuous by boiling. An infusion of nettle leaves, fresh or dried, and sweetened with honey, gives some relief from bronchial congestion.

The rich minerals and iron in nettle leaves make them a valuable vegetable at a time of year when green leaves are in short supply. Expressed juice of the nettle acts as rennet, with salt, in forming curd cheese and junkets.

Nettle beer is an old cottage recipe as a remedy for gout and rheumatic pains, apart from being a pleasant drink. Rheumatic sufferers sometimes chastise themselves by thrashing the affected joints with freshly gathered nettle shoots. The effect is similar to the treatment of rheumatism by bee stings.

The fibre is similar to that of hemp and has been used in the past to make a range of cloths from the finest cambrics to utilitarian cordage and in the manufacture of paper.

Opium poppy *Papaver somniferum* (Papaveraceae)   Annual

The abuse of the product of this plant has led to much human misery, but it has provided one of the greatest painkillers of all time – morphine. Its specific name, *somniferum*, means 'sleep inducing'. Its floppy pink to red flowers are a fine addition to the herb garden, standing well above the glaucous indented leaves. After flowering they dry to produce the 'poppy heads' that are popular with flower arrangers. Propagate from seed sown afresh each spring, although once introduced the plants will seed themselves provided that the soil is not too sticky and cold. In some parts of Britain this poppy is a common wild plant, and seed is readily available. There are double and single flowered forms, in pink, mauve and dull red.

Add it to a representative medicinal collection of herbs. Until recently the seed heads were sold powdered to be used as an infusion for the relief of strains and bruised joints.

Orris *Iris florentina* (Liliaceae)   Perennial
White flower de luce, Florentine iris

The white purple-veined flowers of *Iris florentina* bloom early in the summer and once over the flower stems should be cut back to encourage complete ripening of the root or rhizome – the source of orris. Once the roots are mature in August and September they can be lifted, washed free of soil and dried, after which they adopt the fragrance reminiscent of violets. When they are first lifted they are inodorous, but the scent develops and increases by keeping. This is why the chopped or ground root is so valuable in the making of pot-pourri because it absorbs the homogeneous aroma of all the other ingredients and helps to stabilise the whole perfume.

The plants reach some 2 feet (610 mm) in height and prefer a light soil and sunshine, but with some shade in the course of the day. Propagation is by division of rhizomes in July to September, preferably the former, when the task is much easier. By September more roots have grown, making the tangle more difficult to sort out properly.

Parsley *Petroselinum crispum* (Umbelliferae)   Biennial

Parsley takes pride of place in British kitchens as a garnishing plant, and often one finds the garnish discarded at the end of the meal. Most people do not realise that the crisply curled leaves can be eaten as a salad. Apart from being chopped in the making of parsley sauce to serve with fish and boiled bacon, parsley is an ingredient in *sauce tartare* and in *sauce verte* and *bouquet garni* requires parsley stalk. French housewives tend to add a pinch or two of parsley in much the same way that the British housewife adds salt. The best forms to grow are the richly curly-leaved ones: they are richer in vitamins and iron as well as looking better at the table. Parsley does not dry well but can be frozen after blanching, and although when defrosted it is not so attractive for its usual rôle of garnishing it can be used in all the other ways.

It is a true biennial plant, originating from the regions around the Black Sea. It is best sown in April or May, either in rows or as an edging to garden beds, or even in blocks. Germination can be intolerably slow, and there is a belief that parsley goes nine times to the devil and back before germinating. It can be encouraged a little by soaking the seed overnight before sowing and running along the drill with a kettle of boiling water, just trickling from the spout, immediately before sowing the seed. Where good foliage is needed, do not allow the plants to bolt or flower.

Purslane *Portulaca oleraceae* (Portulacaceae)   Annual

Purslane is a sprawling half-hardy plant that revels in sunshine. The reddish stems and clear green fresh leaves can be used in salads or steamed as a vegetable. Older leaves make a useful addition to stews and soups, and the stems are pickled, in sections, and used as a relish. Both this and *Portulaca sativa*, the golden purslane, are half-hardy annuals and should be sown out of doors in early May once the soil is warming up a bit. Keep the young plants growing, once they are established, by watering judiciously to ensure good quick growth and a better leaf texture. By pinching out the flower buds and preventing the plants from flowering, better leaf growth is maintained and the leaves are discouraged from becoming coarse. The golden purslane seems to need more encouragement, especially in poor summers, but is the more decorative plant to use for the table.

Rampion *Campanula rapunculus* (Campanulaceae)   Biennial
    Several plants seem to be tagged rampion, but the true one has hairbell-like deep blue flowers and is sometimes grown as an ornamental border plant. Previously rampion was cultivated regularly in the kitchen garden as a root vegetable, the root being lifted at the end of the second year. It was eaten cooked and served with a white sauce or sliced thinly and dressed with a vinaigrette as a salad accompaniment.
    The rosette of leaves is formed the first summer, and if the plants are needed for use flower spikes must be prevented from forming in the second summer. By earthing up in the second spring the young leaves are rendered more tender, and it is reported that this also makes the roots a better flavour, preventing any light from coarsening the crown.

Rosemary *Rosmarinus officinalis* (Labiatae)   Perennial
    Rosemary is said to have been a 'comforter of the brains and a strengthener of the memory'. The delicate blue flowers cover the plumes of dark green growth in early summer, and in early seasons or early districts can begin to flower in March. The plants are evergreen and decorative, reaching 5 to 6 feet (1.5 to 1.8 m) in height, and are useful as a hedge plant, although uneven in growth. They tolerate clipping. A sunny site with good drainage is ideal, but the plant is fairly accommodating and can be grown in containers, making it useful for porch plant arrangements in the colder areas. The foliage is richly resinous but has to be brushed with the hand to release the volatile oils.
    Propagation is from cuttings of non-flowering shoots taken in early autumn and put under a cloche or in a sheltered frame to overwinter. Cuttings taken in spring are very successful and can often be encouraged to root in water.
    When rosemary is used as a culinary herb, there will inevitably be some dissension. The flavour is too fierce for many palates, and for this reason it is best to use rosemary leaves after drying,

when some of the pungency has been lost. A sprig or two are often pushed into lamb before roasting, to flavour it, but if a few sprigs are placed beneath the joint while cooking the flavour seems to pervade the whole joint, less strongly and perhaps more evenly. Rosemary leaves are always removed after cooking, and before serving the food, because they are tough and spiky.

Oil of rosemary used to be used as an embrocation for sprained or gouty joints and as an insect repellent. Its long association with hair cosmetics dates back many years to when it was considered effective as a hair restorer. For a refreshing bath, fasten a few sprigs of fresh rosemary into an old nylon stocking and hang it below the taps so that as the water runs into the bath it becomes scented with rosemary.

Always add a dried sprig to pot-pourri; it is one of the main ingredients, but never add too much as its camphorous aroma can overpower any sweet-scented mixture.

Rue *Ruta graveolens* (Rutaceae)   Perennial
Herb of grace

The herb of repentance, rue is an evergreen sub-shrub that forms a rounded bush, the foliage of which is very pungently bitter in aroma when crushed. Its only possible use as a healing herb nowadays is in the treatment of poultry. There is some association with witches and black magic as it was used in the treatment of epilepsy and considered to be a cure for insanity. But rue is an example of a herb being used on conditions that were not understood in the past, and because of its drastic effects in unpractised hands it was thought to possess supernatural powers.

In Tudor times it was commonly strewn in dwellings and public buildings, such as courtrooms, as a protection against evil. In the middle ages its powerful bitterness of flavour was used to mask putrefaction. A leaf or two only, finely chopped, can be added to cream cheese, but beware – a heavy hand with the rue is disastrous.

There are three forms to grow in the decorative herb garden: green, green-blue and variegated-leaved plants. The last often proves difficult to keep as it reverts to its plain green form. The foliage is prettily cut and the four-petalled yellow flowers bloom in summer. Give it a sunny spot with good drainage, for, as with many other herbs from sunnier climes than Britain's, moisture encourages lush growth that is less hardy and inferior in aroma.

Sage *Salvia officinalis* (Labiatae)   Perennial

The culinary sage which is most commonly grown forms a somewhat floppy bush. The leaves are dusty grey in colour, wrinkled and pitted rather like orange peel in appearance, and rough in texture. The whole plant seems rather dry. The leaves are used in making stuffing for poultry and rich meats such as pork and should be gathered before the plant comes into flower. Sage is one of the few herbs that is not usually used fresh but is better dried, because the flavour is then less fierce. Sprigs of leaves can be cut and hung up in loose bunches to dry, in a warm dry atmosphere. Cover them with a piece of cloth or newspaper to keep the sun away if a shaded place cannot be found. Miraculously, sage leaves do not reabsorb moisture even if they are not dried completely.

Sage ale or beer, drunk cold, is said to dispel many varied ailments and to 'increase cheerfulness'. Sage tea was preferred by the Chinese to their own tea, of which they even bartered three times as much by weight for sage from Dutch merchants. It is made by pouring 1 pint (0.6 litres) of boiling water over 1 ounce (28 g) of dried sage leaves and flavouring with either lemon juice or lemon rind to taste, with a spoonful of honey stirred into it. John Evelyn wrote of it as possessing so many properties 'as that the assiduous use of it is said to render men immortal'. Another use of sage is in the flavouring of Derby sage cheese, when the whole cheese takes on a marbled appearance and a strong rough sage-like flavour. Burned in a chestnut roaster, sage smoke will deodorise animal and cooking smells. Crushed, it can be used as a tooth powder, for those who do not find the dryness of the flavour too strong, and used to remove tobacco and red wine stains from the teeth.

The primary requirement when selecting a sage bush for the garden, if the leaves are destined for culinary use, is to find a plant whose idiosyncrasies match the soil conditions. When sage is well suited to the spot in which it is required to grow, it will produce foliage completely devoid of any bitterness of flavour or 'flatness'. A little patience and trial and error are necessary in establishing the right sage bush in the kitchen garden.

Propagation is from summer cuttings taken with a heel, or by layers pegged down in summer and severed and planted out the following spring. The purple-leaved form *Salvia officinalis* 'Purpurascens' makes a good planting contrast in the herb garden; the young foliage is deep plum purple and it is a much lower growing plant. It can be used in the kitchen, but its main use is in the preparation of pharmaceutical products. There is also a tricolor form, with cream, purple-pink and green foliage, called the painted sage, and there are several golden-leaved forms. These are better retained for herb garden effect rather than for the kitchen. However, the narrow-leaved golden sage, *Salvia icterina,* is of a much sweeter flavour and good for culinary use in turkey stuffings.

Pineapple sage is a different species altogether, *Salvia rutilans,* and is a tender plant, only successful in sheltered gardens and away from cold winds and winter dampness, although it can be maintained from a regular supply of cuttings. The leaves are highly aromatic of pineapple when crushed or rubbed, and deep red flowers are produced in the late summer or even early autumn. It makes a good conservatory or porch plant, where the aromatic leaves can be enjoyed in passing.

Salad burnet *Poterium sanguisorba,* Syn. *Sanguisorba minor*
(Rosaceae)   Perennial
Salad burnet is a pretty and hardy plant, sometimes found wild in Britain, whose leaves remain green in winter. In the garden it makes an attractive edging to beds and its small rounded heads of reddish green flowers at midsummer earn it the local name of blood ball. Remove the flowers to encourage leaf production and maintain a continuous supply of dainty cucumber-flavoured leaves to add to salads. There is no aroma to the leaves.

It was used as a herb in medieval times. The leaves may be chopped and added to cream cheese or summer drinks to impart the somewhat crisp flavour likened to that of cucumber skin. The individual leaves need to be removed from the pink stems, but when used for garnishing the colour contrast is an added attraction.

Santolina *see* Lavender cotton.

Savory *Satureia* species, sometimes *Satureja* (Labiatae)
                                                  Annual and perennial
There are two distinct forms of savory: the winter savory, which is a perennial, *Satureia montana*; and an annual plant, *Satureia hortensis*. Neither seems to be widely grown or much used. The flavour is similar to that of an old thyme, rough, peppery and sharp, especially in winter savory. Propagate winter savory by cuttings or by division of roots in autumn or spring, and a plant can be left for five years before it will require to be replaced. The annual savory can be raised from seed sown in April. Two or three crops can be taken from it and it stands up to clipping fairly well. It is widely used as a seasoning in European cookery to flavour gravies and sauces to accompany meat and is said to aid digestion and reduce flatulence. It used to be the substitute for pepper in past centuries, when pepper was prohibitive in price. It is often said to be served in a sauce with beans, but there seems little evidence of such use.

Sea holly *Eryngium maritimum* (Umbelliferae)   Perennial
Eryngo
The sea holly is a thistle-like plant, with jagged blue-grey leaves, spiked with sharp thorny edges, and protective little prickly

leaves surrounding the metallic blue flowerheads. The plants are grown for their roots, which are long and rich in minerals. They used to be a popular sweetmeat and can be candied in the autumn to add to desserts as a sweetening agent or as a flavouring for jams and jellies. Young flowering shoots are said to be eaten in the same way as asparagus, the prickles being rendered innocuous by boiling.

Sea holly is a lovely plant to grow where there is plenty of sunshine and a light soil, where it has space to spread out unhampered by leafy neighbours.

Propagation is by root division in the autumn or from autumn-sown seed.

Sorrel *Rumex acetosa* (Polygonaceae) Perennial treated as annual

The sorrel grown in our gardens is a good and cultivated form of the wild sorrel, *Rumex acetosa*. It is known also as garden or common sorrel and occasionally even called broad-leaved sorrel. Inevitably there is some confusion because both wild and garden plants are called French sorrel by various authorities.

It is a perennial plant with broad arrow-shaped leaves and spikes of clustered tiny red-brown flowers in summer. The tangy flavour of the leaves is its main culinary attribute but it is only at its best before the plant flowers. So where the leaves are habitually used as salading, it is advisable to nip out the flower buds as soon as they begin to form. The flavour of the leaves is appreciated more by the French than anyone else, and recipes using sorrel can be found in books on French cookery. Sorrel soup is good, or the leaves can be wrapped around meat to tenderise it or around minced and risotto mixtures in the way that vine leaves are used. As an addition to salad, the leaves ought to be chopped and are especially well matched to tomato. Try a sorrel leaf in sandwiches with cold meat, for a refreshing flavour.

Propagation is by seed sown in drills, as for most salad crops, the seedlings being thinned subsequently. At all costs, the plants must be prevented from bolting, and by growing a few in a shaded situation a supply of less coarse leaves will always be available.

Rumex scutatus is a smaller plant altogether, sometimes called the buckler-leaved sorrel, and is lax of habit or even with trailing stems. The leaves are small and a paler green, and their flavour is not so good.

Southernwood *Artemisia abrotanum* (Compositae) Perennial
Old man, lad's love

The rather gnarled and dead appearance of this little bush in winter has gained it the name of old man, but it is the most delightful addition to any herb or fragrant garden. Its soft green feathery foliage is silky to the touch and almost invites one to play with it to release the sweet camphor aroma. The foliage can be dried and added to mixed herbs for scenting cupboards and drawers, or a sprig can be put into a pot-pourri mixture. Plant it where it will be away from the summer winds and where it has some moisture-retentive material around its base. Cut it back early in the spring to encourage fresh growth in summer. It is a non-flowering plant.

Sweet Cicely *Myrrhis odorata* (Umbelliferae)   Perennial

The leaves of sweet Cicely are soft and lacy in texture, the growth appearing early in the spring. Tiny white flowers in May are carried in umbels like those of its numerous relatives and are followed by large black seeds, which have a flavour slightly like that of liquorice. Try them scattered on creams and ice cream or, when unripe, added to salads. The foliage is sweet in flavour and makes a good addition to diabetic diets. It can be stewed with gooseberries or rhubarb or, for its lightness of flavour, chopped into a green salad, with restraint. The leaves do not dry.

Tansy *Tanacetum vulgare* (Compositae)   Perennial

Tansy was used as one of the strewing herbs, because of its insecticide and deodorant qualities, and the dried leaves used to be kept among clothes and in bedding to repel fleas and lice. A loose bunch of tansy leaves hung up in a larder will discourage flies, or tansy leaves rubbed over meat covers will avert the attentions of blowflies.

Formerly it was a popular cleansing spring tonic, and tansy tea or tansy wine was always taken to tone up the system after the stodgy food of the winter. Habitually it was eaten at Easter, mainly in tansy cake or tansy pudding, known as 'tansies', commemorating the bitter herbs of the Passover. It is too strong for most palates and is now not generally recommended for use internally.

As an infusion, the leaves make a good soothing lotion for bathing aching or bruised joints and sprains or as a treatment for varicose veins.

Cultivation is so easy that a gardener might better be advised to keep tansy at bay and constantly pull away the wandering roots. It will march across the garden; whichever spot is chosen for it, it will prefer to be elsewhere. It is a tough-growing perennial plant; the stems are so tough that they cannot be picked easily by hand, but require to be cut with secateurs.

Tarragon *Artemisia dracunculus* (Compositae)   Perennial
Estragon

The true French tarragon is a superior culinary herb, very useful in giving a blunt bite and heightening the flavour of other herbs. At its best it is used in the more sophisticated cookery, being added to egg dishes, fish, tomatoes, herb butters and cream soups. It is perhaps most familiar in tarragon vinegar, where fresh sprigs are put into a bottle filled with white wine vinegar. Allow it to remain for a couple of months, shaking occasionally. Stems to be used in this way are best gathered in the early part of the summer, when the essential oils in the plant are at their best and richest in flavour. Tarragon does not dry well, so it will need to be quick-frozen if it is needed for winter use. Whenever it is not fresh, there is a tendency for the flavour to become somewhat stale.

It is a southern European plant and therefore loves warmth, so grow it in a sunny spot where the drainage is good, to prevent lush growth forming. Otherwise it will succumb to the damp British winter.

Russian tarragon, *Artemisia dracunculoides,* has an inferior flavour and is not recommended for culinary use, although it ought to be included in the collection of culinary herbs for completeness.

Thyme *Thymus vulgaris* (Labiatae)   Perennial
This rather twiggy perennial grows wild in southern Europe on the stony sun-baked hillsides. The tiny leaves are dark green and it is one of those culinary herbs that is used dried or semi-dried on the stalk, because the flavour is too strong when used fresh. They are dried on the stalk because it is then easy to remove the leaves before serving the dish, as they become rather prickly and tough with cooking. But their flavour persists throughout long cooking, and so thyme is particularly useful in the preparation of casseroles and stews, and it is an ingredient of *bouquet garni.* The warm pungent flavour blends very well with that of olives, garlic and tomato, and thyme is very useful in the preparation of such meat as rabbit, hare and game.

Although the best thyme to use is the wild thyme, *Thymus vulgaris,* the lemon thyme, *Thymus* × *citriodorus,* is a useful addition to the cook's armoury of flavour. The clear lemon aroma and taste match sweet dishes well and are good in creamy sauces and fruit desserts or with fish. There is also a tiny-leaved plant called the caraway thyme, *Thymus herba barona,* which was used traditionally for rubbing over the baron of beef to impart its flavour. But all thymes are powerfully aromatic and so need to be used with considerable care, or their flavour can be all pervading.

Thymes need a non-acid soil, sharp drainage and as much sunshine as possible. They are good plants for using as edging to paths, where they can spread and smudge the clear outline. Tuck them between the paving stones of paths where they will be trodden on to release their scent. *Thymus vulgaris* is hummockforming and so are its forms 'Aureus', with golden foliage, and 'Variegatus', with variegated leaves. Both forms have retained the fragrance. The caraway thyme, on the other hand, is creeping and carpet-forming, where its hairy leaves can survive the winter dampness.

Valerian *Valeriana officinalis* (Valerianaceae)   Perennial
Phew, phu plant

A herb of ancient cultivation known to Arab physicians, valerian was grown for its useful rootstock, still listed in some pharmacopoeias. The root is roughly conical, with fibrous creeping offshoots when matured at the end of the summer. It is not lifted until about November when all the top growth has died down, for as long as this is green it is helping to enrich and mature the root. Once lifted, the roots need to be washed free of soil, and if they are bruised they develop an offensive smell, which has earned the plant its vernacular name of 'phew'. The smell is likened to that of old leather and is said to attract vermin and cats.

Grown in the herb garden, for its pretty, tall flowering stems with trimly cut leaflets, it is a good plant for the back of the border. Put it where it will get some shade during the day, or in the dappled light beneath overhanging trees.

The flowers are very pale pink, in tight clustered heads in midsummer. The whole plant has a slightly foetid smell, but if it is at the back of the border there will be no temptation to touch it in passing, and its upstanding decorative quality certainly earns it a place in the herb garden. Propagate it by dividing the rootstock – and tolerating the smell for a few minutes.

This is not the plant so commonly grown as valerian, *Centranthus rubra,* of coastal regions.

Veratrum *Veratrum album* (Liliaceae)   Perennial
White hellebore

At first glance this plant is sometimes confused with the yellow gentian, but a distinguishing feature is that the ribbed pleated leaves of the veratrum are alternate up the stem, whereas the gentian has opposite leaves. It is a statuesque plant, upstanding and quite imposing with its broad leaves and greenish white flowers in summer. This and the other hellbores (green and black) are strong poisons, formerly thought to have magical powers and surrounded by fear and superstitions. They have all been used as a dip for poison arrows. All of them irritate the skin and can cause blistering, but *album* especially is a dramatic plant to include in a herb garden. It needs a fairly well worked deep soil with some moisture-retentive material down at the roots and, once established, will look after itself.

Verbena, Lemon-scented *see* Lemon verbena

Vervain *Verbena officinalis* (Verbenaceae)   Perennial
Vervain has long been associated with magic and sorcery and came to be one of the most important sacred herbs used in the making of holy salves. Its somewhat washed-out lilac flowers, appearing intermittently from about June to September in spikes, have little decorative quality, but vervain has a place in collections because of the medical folklore associated with it.

As a soothing wash for bruising or to cool the forehead in times of sickness, it is still used. An infusion is sometimes recommended for washing wounds.

The Victorians seem to have used it widely for a variety of home remedies, not least as a hair tonic. One of the first proprietary hair tonics to be marketed was made from vervain. Herbalists used to sell it as a soothing eye wash, especially for scrofulous eye conditions.

Violet *Viola odorata* (Violaceae)   Perennial
Sweet violet
The violet has been a symbol of constancy since ancient times, when it was used as an officinal plant and as a cosmetic – the dye was used to paint the eyelids. In the nineteenth century it was one of the most popular of flowers used in love tokens, and Napoleon is said to have bestowed a nosegay of violets upon Josephine for each wedding anniversary.

Over the centuries, the leaves have formed poultices and dressings for ulcers and wounds of different kinds and have been used as a cure for insomnia, gout, cardiac complaints, a soothing remedy for headaches, a laxative, a treatment for catarrh and bronchitis, a gargle for sore throats, and in the relief of rheumatic pains – in fact it seems to have been a general cure-all.

Flowers can be candied and used in confectionery, and the favourite French *vyolette* became a recipe used in England at the time of the Restoration; macerated boiled violet flowers were used to impart colour to rice flour, which was then boiled with milk and sugar. Sometimes this is known as 'violet paste' and was supposed to be endowed with remarkable health-giving properties.

Before synthetic perfumes were manufactured following the First World War, violet water and sweet violet perfume were amongst the most popular scents, although often adulterated by the rhizome of the Florentine iris, *Iris florentina*. It is remarkable that at first the flowers smell delightfully sweet, and then the fragrance fades immediately. This is because it virtually anaesthetises the nasal nerves.

In the garden, sweet violets like best to be left to themselves in a shady bank, just as in their wild state. They are stoloniferous and mat-forming where they are happy.

Woad *Isatis tinctoria* (Cruciferae)   Biennial
Dyer's woad

The blue dye obtained from the woad plant seems surprisingly inappropriate, for the plant has profuse bright yellow flowers. The dye known from ancient times is obtained by fermenting the bruised leaves, but nowadays its use as a wool dye has been superseded. However, leaves picked during the first year of growth can be put to use.

Grow woad from seed sown in autumn as soon as it is ripe. In good summers, the rich black seeds ripen beautifully in southern British gardens, decking the plant with shining black beads. It germinates easily, develops into a good rosette the first year and flowers the second.

Woodruff *Asperula odorata* (Rubiaceae)   Perennial

A plant of the woods and other shaded localities, woodruff has white star-like flowers and a straggling habit. Once dried, it takes on the scent of new-mown hay, which strengthens with time. For this reason alone it is invaluable as an ingredient of pot-pourri, scented sachets and herb pillows. It is also useful to spread about in closed bookcases to remove and avoid mustiness. The persistent scent means that woodruff can be used as a perfume fixative.

Propagation is by division of the running roots, in autumn. It can look rather weedy when not in flower but is such a simple plant that no garden should be without a patch.

6. Plan to use herbs

Herbs in various proportions, alone or in a mixture, are used in culinary practice to enhance flavour, to garnish, or to aid the digestion of rich dishes. It is essential to use some herbs fresh – or, if not, at least to accept that when they are frozen or dried their effect will be inferior to that of the fresh form. Such culinary herbs are fennel, chervil, parsley and basil. When mint is to be used to make mint sauce there is no possibility of using dried leaves but, on the other hand, when dried it is used in stuffings, pilaffs or soups to lend a more strident flavour, such as is needed in Middle Eastern cookery.

Some herbs are habitually used dried and not as a substitute for fresh ones, chiefly because the bite of their flavour is reduced by drying and their pungency becomes more acceptable. Such herbs are bay, rosemary, sage and thyme, although lemon thyme is at its most delicious when fresh.

Herbs in cooking

A *bouquet garni*, which appears in many recipes, is a small bunch or bouquet of mixed herbs tied together. The composition varies with the kind of dish being prepared, and it is usual to tie the little bunch to the side of the cooking utensil and remove and discard it before serving. Commercially, small muslin bags, similar to tea bags, are available; although inferior and invariable, they can be used in a similar way when fresh herbs are not forthcoming. In general, a *bouquet garni* for use in preparing poultry or game recipes might be a couple of sprigs of dried thyme, a stalk or two of fresh parsley and a bay leaf. A general *bouquet garni* for use with meat cooked slowly is a stalk or two of dried thyme, stems of fresh parsley, one of marjoram, one of dried rosemary, a bay leaf and an inch or two of celery or lovage stem. A *bouquet garni* can be small or large according to taste and for a wide variety of dishes it can be made up to individual taste from: parsley, savory, rosemary, tarragon, burnet, chervil, celery, basil, thyme and bay leaf.

Fines herbes are a mixture of chopped herbs, such as parsley, chives, tarragon and chervil, cooked in the recipe and left in when served. The term is generally used, especially on menus, to mean chopped parsley, which is the only herb added to many *omelettes aux fines herbes*.

Tussie-mussies

A custom of ancient refinement was the giving of a nosegay to personages of elevated rank or profession who had to enter somewhat unsavoury buildings or mix with unclean prisoners or sick persons. These nosegays have been variously called tussie-mussy, tusmore or tussemore and although of no utilitarian purpose in the twentieth century they make charming little gifts and can be hung in cupboards for short-term effectiveness or just put in tiny vases on the dressing table or bedside table to sweeten the air. They can be made in various ways, usually with a rosebud as the centre piece and artemisia, lemon thyme, lavender, geranium and santolina fastened around to form a tiny Victorian posy-like bunch. Fastened with a gay ribbon or backed by a frill of paper, they are a near-useless bit of enchanting nonsense.

Pot-pourri

Recipes for pot-pourri vary: some of the old ones are reliable, many more recent ones vague and some rather complicated, presenting problems and expense in acquiring the recommended extracts and essences. Essentially pot-pourri is a homogeneous mixture of dried scented flower petals and aromatic leaves together with some spices, and no single perfume should predominate. In general proportions, the most successful recipes appear to combine one part leaves to seven parts flower petals with small amounts of spices and citrus peels. Flowers with thick fleshy petals like lilies, although strongly scented, are unsuitable. Flowers and leaves need to be gathered in the middle of the day or in the afternoon when they are quite dry and free of both rain and dew, and when the blossoms are just coming to their prime. Roses ought to be picked before they are fully out, but this is a sacrifice few of us can make, and petals from red roses appear to dry better than other rose petals. Pluck the petals individually from the flowerhead and spread them out on newspaper, cloth or in a garden sieve (not plastic sheeting) in a shady place to dry. The time required to get them dry and papery to the touch varies according to the moisture content of the different kinds. Other sweet-scented flowers can be treated in the same way, in lesser quantities, but rose petals form the bulk basis of a satisfactory pot-pourri and old fashioned roses are even better. Suitable flowers to include are carnations, pinks, honeysuckle, lavender, mock orange, mignonette, stocks, sweet peas and other sweet smelling flowers. Several of the wild herbs may be used, especially those used for strewing in days gone by, like woodruff, lady's bedstraw and clover. The aromatic leaves, without stalk, to include are those of lavender, rosemary, marjoram, verbena, southernwood, scented geraniums and sweet bay. These need to be either dried and rubbed through a fine sieve or minced and dried on paper for some hours before incorporating them in a recipe.

To prepare the citrus peel, which is usually lemon peel though some recipes call for orange peel as well, pare the fruits very finely, avoiding all the white pith. Then dry the peel in a warming drawer or put it on a baking tray in the oven when the cooking is finished and the oven has been turned off. Once dry the peel can be finely minced.

Pot-pourri, literally translated from the French, means 'rotten pot', and in the early days of pot-pourri making flowers and other plant material were virtually pickled and kept moist. Such a 'preserve' remains richly aromatic over many years and is usually kept in closed containers, opened only infrequently, when a room is to be perfumed. This kind of pot-pourri is known as moist pot-pourri.

Dry pot-pourri is less arduous to make and is more popular today, when it is enjoyed in open bowls about the house or in pot-pourri containers with holes in the lid to allow the scented air to circulate. Dry mixtures are not so long lasting.

The art of pot-pourri making has developed and changed as new fragrant plants have been introduced to Britain's gardens through the centuries. Modern recipes can be contrived or controlled to be herby, spicy, aromatic or sweet, by blending the ingredients, but many of the basic plants remain those that were used first in Elizabethan days. Many herbs can be included, such as lavender, chamomile, bergamot, catmint, lily-of-the-valley, myrtle, mignonette, lemon balm, lemon verbena, thyme, southernwood, santolina, apple mint, pineapple sage, muscatel sage, bay, broom, marjoram, hyssop, orris root and elecampane root.

Gardening with herbs

Today the making of a 'flowery mead' or natural area where wild flowers grow in the garden is a deliberate conservation exercise. The fashion is evolving as good horticultural practice, certainly as a cultural challenge. Many of the wild plants included are native herbs, the very plants that were brought into cultivation several hundred years ago. When the monks planted 'flowery meads' they were probably indulging their delight in wild flowers, and through the centuries these 'simples' were collected from the fields and hedgerows for use, or brought into collections for cultivation.

Particularly during the past two decades numerous traditional herbs have had to be sought out and brought back into commercial availability in response to the demands of natural cuisine, pure cosmetics, alternative medicine and veterinary science. Consequently, quite unwittingly, a vast conservation exercise has been undertaken. Simultaneously, the fashion for decorative herb gardens, and the consequent updating of knowledge and affirmation of identity has bestowed a respectability upon herbs. No longer are they shrouded in legend as ancestral curios, the cult of cranks; they are now at the forefront of both horticulture and medicine — back where they were three hundred years ago.

Representative collections have been made in many gardens, both large and small. The National Trust has created herb gardens of varying styles in some gardens under their guardianship. The Royal Horticultural Society acknowledged the vogue in 1977-78 when they made a formal herb garden at Wisley. Nowadays we all have our favourites, be they in public parks, gardens sometimes open to the public, cathedral precincts or a neighbouring plot. Using herbs, respecting them and continuing to cultivate them ensures their conservation.

Herb suppliers

Arne Herbs, Limeburn Nurseries, Limeburn Hill, Chew Magna, Avon BS18 8QW. Telephone: 0272 333399.

Cosby House Herbs, Croft Road, Leicester LE9 5RE. Telephone: 0533 864261.

Devon Herbs, Burn Lane, Brentor, Tavistock, Devon PL19 0ND. Telephone: 082281 285.

Heches Herbs, St Peter-in-the-Wood, Guernsey, Channel Isles. Telephone: 0481 63545. Lecture holidays.

Herbs in Stock, Whites Hill, Stock, Ingatestone, Essex. Telephone: 0277 841130.

Hollington Nurseries Ltd, Woolton Hill, Newbury, Berkshire RG15 9XT. Telephone: 0635 253908.

John Chambers, 15 Westleigh Road, Barton Seagrave, Kettering, Northamptonshire NN15 5AJ. Telephone: 0933 681632. Wild flower seed specialist.

Lathbury Park Herb Garden, Newport Pagnell, Buckinghamshire MK16 8LD. Telephone: 0908 610316.

Norfolk Lavender Ltd, Caley Mill, Heacham, King's Lynn, Norfolk PE31 7JE. Telephone: 0485 70384.

Old Rectory Herb Garden, Ightham, near Sevenoaks, Kent. Telephone: 0732 882608.

Samares Herbs a Plenty, Samares Manor, St Clement, Jersey, Channel Isles. Telephone: 0534 70551.

Selsey Herb and Goat Farm, Waterlane, Selsey, Stroud, Gloucestershire. Telephone: 04536 6682.

Suffolk Herbs Ltd, Sawyers Farm, Little Cornard, Sudbury, Suffolk. Telephone: 0787 227247.

Thornham Herbs, The Walled Garden, Thornham Magna, Eye, Suffolk IP23 8HA. Telephone: 037983 510.

Yorkshire Herbs, The Herb Centre, Middleton Tyas, Richmond, North Yorkshire. Telephone: 032577 686.

Herb gardening courses

Brinsbury College of Agriculture and Horticulture, Brinsbury, North Heath, Pulborough, West Sussex RH20 1DL. Telephone: 07982 5222.

Cosby House Herbs, Cosby House, Croft Road, Cosby, Leicestershire LE9 5RE. Telephone: 0533 864261.

Gardening courses in Somerset, The Garden Form, Riverside Place, St James Street, Taunton, Somerset TA1 1JH.

Farnham Royal Herbs, Farnham Court, Church Road, Farnham Royal, Buckinghamshire SL2 3AW.

English Gardening School, Chelsea Physic Garden, 66 Royal Hospital Road, Chelsea, London SW3 4HS. Telephone: 01 352 4347.

Index